AHEAD OF THE CURVE

*An intimate conversation with women
in the second half of life*

BONNIE B. MATHESON

Ahead of the Curve
An intimate conversation with women in the second half of life

Published by Wheatmark®
610 East Delano Street, Suite 104
Tucson, Arizona 85705 U.S.A.
www.wheatmark.com

International Standard Book Number: 978-1-60494-289-7
Library of Congress Control Number: 2009927417

For more information go to www.IBetYouCan.net.

*This book is dedicated to my mother
Ruth Hale Buchanan.
She has been my inspiration all of my life.
Because of her youthfulness and vitality I have never
feared aging.
I love you, Mother!*

"You can learn and change and grow, because you are literally making a new brain every day. Since you sat down in your seat here tonight, you've made thousands of new neurons! You are literally being given the opportunity to think new thoughts, to change your mind, to create the reality you experience, from moment to moment. It's no longer just a truism that thinking positively is a good idea—thank you, Dr. Norman Vincent Peale! If you think positive thoughts, you are building a very different brain than if you think negative thoughts."

—Candace Pert, PhD
Author of *Everything You Need to Know to Feel Good*
and *Molecules of Emotion*

ACKNOWLEDGMENTS

I want to thank so many people who helped me get this project off the ground. It all started with my friend Susie Saunders who sent me an outline based on my words in a phone conversation we had about women over fifty. She emailed it to me saying, "Use this to start your book." That is exactly what I did.

I knew I would need someone to stand by me while I spent months interviewing women all over the country. Nancy Marriott acted as my book coach. Everyone needs a book coach. Without her encouragement and patience I would never have begun to flesh out those outline ideas. Rachel Cartwright edited and reedited through some very unsettled times in my life, including a romance that did not work out and a move to a new part of the state.

Mary Wolfe was a rock. Her sense of humor often kept me going. Tiffany Snider transcribed all those many interviews from tapes to digital words. What would I have done without her? Melanie Smart gave me positive energy and showed me how much personal growth can happen in a short span of time.

Jenni Bowman gave me such wonderful support in the final weeks. I hate to think what would have happened without her.

Dr. Walter Bortz, and many other physicians with whom I spoke to verify some statements about health, inspired me to take my own line. So many others helped to give me a sense of aging in our time. There are simply too many to name. So thank you to all of you who have spoken with me, called me, emailed me, and let me interview you. I could never have finished this book without you.

To my family a very special thank you. I know many of you wish I had decided to use a pen name. But I also know that you all understand that being true to myself is part of the message of this book. I am happy to accept responsibility for my own actions. I love you all so much it would take an entire book to express my feelings.

CONTENTS

INTRODUCTION

I guess I could have curled up into a little ball and closed my mind and heart to the world. I guess I could have been discouraged and defeated. But I was not. In fact, I was energized and excited.

It all started on a fall day in 2003.

On that day, I began my journey. I spent $200 at the market and came home with a couple of bags of extremely healthy food and three bunches of roses. It was a gentle beginning. And I had a lovely day and evening cocktails with friends. I did not tell them that my husband had just left our house for the last time. I did not mention that my 42-year marriage was over. I did something I had never done before. I invited friends without first checking with my husband. I picked people whom *I* liked, never worrying about whether he liked them or not. It was liberating and reassuring to me to have had such a nice time that evening.

All my life, I'd expected to stay married forever. Divorce was simply not an option. Yet, it happened almost of its own volition. My husband and I were married when we were both 19 years old. What seemed to be a lasting love did not last. But our friendship has remained.

Many people have asked us why we "bothered" to divorce at our ages. But that is exactly the point I am making in this book. We both expect to live another 30 years or more and simply like each other too well to impose that 30 years on each other. We agreed it was time for us to have other lives, other relationships, and so we set each other free to pursue our dreams individually.

One man changed my life with a simple story he told me about his disappointment for not having followed his dream. He was my grandfather-in-law. He used to tell me that he had always wanted to become a doctor. He wanted this very much, but he was busy with his family. Life simply grew too complicated. When he was 40, he considered going to medical school, but he bowed to the conventional wisdom that said he was too old. His wife and four children expected him to act responsibly and that meant keeping to a predictable, conventional life.

I loved this man. He was a wonderful grandfather to his many grandchildren and a wonderful role model. He was short; small of stature. His blue eyes sparkled, and his full mustache reminded me of a Jack Russell terrier. When he spoke, he had a slight Scottish brogue, even though he and his father before him were born in the United States. He was proud of his Scottish ancestry. He taught me to call those from Scotland by the name "Scots" or use the term "Scottish," but never, ever to use the term "Scotch" to describe a man from Scotland.

"*Scotch* is a drink!" he would say emphatically, his cane tapping a rhythm on the floor. We all paid attention when he reacted in this manner.

One day, he spoke seriously to me about what happened to his dream of going to medical school. He said, "If I had gone to medical school at 40, I would have completely finished whatever I needed to do, even internships, by 50. By now, I could have practiced for 25 years or so." He was over 75 years old when we had this conversation. He added, looking me right in the eyes, "Never let anyone tell you that you are too old to do anything. It just isn't true."

This was the most important gift he ever gave me.

For some reason, that conversation stayed with me. I never forgot it. In fact, I remembered it vividly when I decided to attend college at age 50. I knew many people would tease me. One of my sisters-in-law said, "Now *there* is a midlife crisis if I ever saw one!" And maybe she was more correct than either of us knew at the time. But I never called it a crisis. Honestly, for me it was a courageous endeavor, and I was at first terrified to begin it.

There was another reason that I felt comfortable with my decision to return to school. Yet another authority figure had bestowed advice on me when I was in a receptive mood. When I was 47 years old, I arrived for one of my semi-annual checkups at my gynecologist's office. He talked to me at each visit in a way that I think few medical doctors have time to do anymore. He knew everything about me and my family for three generations.

This day he changed the course of my life with a few words that became unexpectedly significant, as it turned out. My doctor told me that women of my generation who were vaccinated, well-nourished, and educated about keeping healthy would have a 33% chance of living to be 100 years old.

"I don't want to be an old lady of 100!" I exclaimed emphatically. But he smiled and pointed a finger directly at me as he replied, "Whether you want to or not, nevertheless, you have a 33% chance of doing so!"

Again, that conversation stayed with me. Even though I discounted it at the time, it wedged itself into my subconscious. When I approached my 50th birthday, I began to think in terms of having 50 more years. It certainly changed my perception of aging. Most of my friends were wringing their hands and saying, "Oh, dear! Oh, dear!" They felt that their lives were winding down and that it was too late to make changes now.

But unlike them, I felt that I had ages to do all I wished to do in the future. After all, in the preceding 50 years I realized I had grown up, finished high school, married, had five children, moved several times, made my way as a hostess in my community, started a career in real estate, served on numerous boards of directors and many, many other things. It seemed realistic to plan to accomplish much more in the following 50 years, because now I had the added wisdom of the first 50 years to help me complete all my goals in the second half of my life.

Many goals presented themselves. Because I had married so young and immediately began having babies, I only completed one semester of college. I wanted to go back to college and earn a degree. The reason I wanted to do that was so I would be prepared to earn a Ph.D. I felt I needed those credentials in order to be taken seriously by doctors. I have wanted to be on equal footing with physicians for many years because I have some very strong opinions about what they do. Earning my degree had seemed like something that would take too long when I was younger, but by age 50, I realized the time in school would pass very quickly.

I also wanted to regain my figure and shed the many pounds put on after stopping smoking. Before my revelation, the effort seemed just too great. But by 50, I knew I had the time to take it slowly and just let it happen naturally, as I ate a more healthy diet and continued to exercise daily.

I also wanted to write a book about childbirth. But at that time, I did not believe that I could because I was afraid I did not have the credibility to be taken seriously. There are often such flimsy ideas stopping us from doing what we wish. Do not let anyone tell you that you cannot do something. Try. You *will* surprise yourself. And you may surprise a few other people, too.

I realize now that very often things are moved forward by people who are not necessarily specialists in a field, but rather who carry a passion for changing something or helping people. It is not necessary to know everything. No one does. But having a passion for a subject makes studying it more fun. You will be amazed how much your mind can absorb if you try. At any rate, I later found myself becoming the CEO of a company solely devoted to childbirth. No one has ever questioned my passion.

Childbirth has been an enduring passion of mine as long as I can remember. When I was four, my mother gave birth to a baby boy. She went to the hospital and came home with a baby. Everyone made a big fuss over her and the baby. I liked that. A few months later I went to the hospital to have my tonsils removed. I excitedly told everyone that I planned to go to the hospital and bring home a baby, and everyone in my family and extended family played along with me. They gave me flowers in a little vase shaped like a bassinette, and I brought home a life-size baby doll from the hospital. It seemed very romantic to me.

Later, when I began to understand where babies came from, I felt it would be the prime sexual act to have a baby. For some reason, giving birth always made me feel complete. I *knew* that I wanted to have a baby, probably several, and started out with a typical hospital birth for my first child. In those days the hospital was considered the modern and the safe place to have a baby. Even though I knew that both my mother and my father were born at home, I did not think of my home as the place to go to birth a baby.

Later I became adept at having babies and an expert on the subject of natural childbirth. I learned to my chagrin that doctors do not know more about my body (or anyone's body) than I do. It came as a shock to me to learn this. In fact, for many years I felt somehow guilty about this knowledge. Now I feel militant about it. Having my babies changed me. First of all it made me "grow up and do it myself." My first baby—when I was barely 20—entered the world while I was gassed unconscious. I was put to sleep only after some hours of terror and pain, having given over all of my power to the "experts" in the hospital, and I was helpless. I felt alone and full of fear.

No one let me know that I was powerful. No one said to me, *You can do this*. In fact, everyone led me to believe that without them I would never get it done. Or I would die. There was no concept of trusting the natural act of birth. Birth was treated as a disease to be dealt with by professionals.

I no longer believe this. Nature designed us women to make babies in our bodies, and we know how to get them out of our bodies as well. However, that is an entirely different book, so I will spare you the details at this time. Suffice it to say, that I began to work on my own personal growth due to having babies. I learned a lot about myself through the act of childbirth. I knew that part of the reason for success with childbirth was due to attitude. In fact, I believe that all of what happens to us in life is dependent on our attitude about it.

Years earlier, I had watched my father gradually eat himself alive from the inside out with the negativity he had about a lot of people. In spite of the fact that in many ways he was a wonderful, generous and gregarious man, he had some fatal flaws. He was vengeful and prejudiced, and it made him sick.

As a child I heard sermons in church which said that anger and resentment could destroy us. My father's example proved this to me. I am not completely certain about the nature of forgiveness and good health, but I *know* it works if one can remain optimistic and positive. I am determined to stay positive and optimistic and forgiving, if for no other reason than to maintain my good health. No anger or resentment will eat me alive. I am vigilant about my thinking and always try to rout out negative thoughts before they can take root.

In writing this book, I hope to heal my own childhood traumas or feelings of inadequacy instilled in me by the negative people around me. Somehow, I rose above the verbal abuse of a woman who was charged with my care as my nanny. She was a sad woman who had lost two baby boys at birth. She hovered about my life like a black cloud of negativity and fear. But I never totally believed that I was as worthless as she said I was. I had grave doubts, of course, because I had been taught to respect my elders, and it was difficult to tell myself that she was wrong.

It took years to erase the damage done to my self confidence. Having babies helped me to do that. When I realized that power of my body, it amazed me—I could barely believe it. But I had to believe it, because I had the living proof. I had my children. Gradually that confidence built a strong inner core of peace and self-knowledge. I have never looked back.

It worked so effectively that I have since tried hard to give other women the gift of knowing their own bodies' natural power. Because of my desire to help women find themselves, I started a company, Childbirth Solutions Inc. Even though that company was never financially successful, I have had the immense satisfaction of having many, many women come up to me and say, "You changed my life!"

Over the years, such responses from women have been

among my greatest joys. Knowing I have made a difference in the lives of others has helped erase the painful memories of my first birthing experience and inspired me to reach out and empower women wherever I can.

No one knows what the future holds. The important thing to know is that no matter what happens, you can handle it. Like me, you can stay ahead of the curve.

Today, I consider myself successful in my mission. All of my accomplished goals have made it possible for me to look to the future with hope and anticipation, rather than with fear.

I feel I have been given the gift of optimism. It is also my gift to you that you may fulfill your own success, and live the second half of your life *ahead of the curve.*

CHAPTER 1

THE BEST 50 YEARS

And the day came when the risk to remain tight in a bud
was more painful than the risk it took to blossom.

—ANAIS NIN (1903–1977)

Are you growing in your life?

As a mid-life woman, do you anticipate challenges, take on new adventures, and inquire deeply into yourself on a regular basis?

Are you living your life *ahead of the curve*, in action with all of your most ardent desires, hopes and dreams, or do you spin out along the wayside, lost in a life that is going nowhere?

If you failed to answer a resounding "*Yes*" to these questions, then welcome aboard. This book is for you.

But only if you want to change.

KNOW WHAT YOU WANT

One of my favorite sayings is: *Evolve, don't revolve.* There is much to be said about a life of personal growth versus a life of going around in circles endlessly, stuck in the same old patterns. But that enlightened exhortation makes even more sense today than ever before.

As baby boomer women—the vast number of us born between 1946 and 1964—we are challenged with a profound shift in consciousness in this, the first decade of the 21st century. We have come of age. Old ideas about aging, relationships, and careers are dropping by the wayside as we reinvision and reinvent ourselves for a future that our mothers never imagined possible.

Such a shift in what we can expect points up to the need for a new action plan for a second half of life. That second half begins at about the half-century mark. Better throw out the rocking chair and get started on getting clear about what you really want and how you are going to get it.

To begin with, ask yourself, "*What is missing from my life?*" Too often, we ask what is *wrong* with my life, or if we ask what is missing, it is with a sense of negativity. That is not a very useful approach. Instead, look at what is missing that would make the biggest difference and truly enhance the quality of your life. Put aside your judgments about whatever it might be—a lover, world travel, a career, an achievement. It doesn't matter whether it's right or wrong, good or bad, possible or impossible.

Another way to approach getting clear about what you want is to answer this question: Do you have some secret or not-so-secret desires that you would like to fulfill in your lifetime? Your desires have probably been secret because you think it's too late, and you've become resigned that you can't have what you want. Some of them are so secret, you've all but forgotten what they are! But here is the good news: It is *not* too late! All it takes is you being willing to bring those secret desires out into the light of day.

Exactly what are those things that you still want to do? As they surface in your memory, get out a paper and pen and write them down. Elaborate and refine them. Know them in your heart and mind. Make them real. Do not think of them as hopeless, even if they are not practical. The very act of making them conscious rather than hidden is magical, and you never know what shape those secret dreams may take now to fulfill you and bring you joy.

My experience illustrates how unearthing secret desires and letting them find expression in your life can work, often in a surprising way. I always wanted to be a ballerina when I was a little girl. After several years of ballet lessons, it became apparent that my body simply was not designed for professional ballet. For many years, I mourned that dream that had come to dust. I even bought a pair of toe shoes and put them on my feet now and then, just to see how I might have looked. I loved those toe shoes.

Years passed. I grew up and married. When I had daughters, I wondered if either of them would want to dance. Would they be able to? Neither one of them seemed to be budding ballerinas, though. We lived in the rural countryside, and classes were few and very far between. So I gave up on my dream. But somewhere in the back of my mind, it was still simmering.

I have a very strong belief in the theory that we get what we focus our minds on. But I have never considered myself an expert in this—just lucky. It amazes me how many of the things I focused on as my "heart's desires" when I was young have actually come true. Sometimes these wishes manifest in ways I never would have thought of. But the pleasure is the same, if not more so, because of the way they actually presented themselves.

I was newly separated from my husband when my sister-in-law asked me to a performance of the Washington Ballet at the Kennedy Center in Washington DC, near my home in Virginia. I was enchanted. I had of course been to the ballet a few times during my 42-year marriage, but always with my husband. I remember being acutely aware of his boredom and desire to leave early. So I watched with only half my brain and never fully relaxed into the full experience. It was a revelation to me to go with someone who, like me, really wanted to be there. I will never forget my joy that night. And I will be forever grateful to my sister-in-law, Janis Buchanan, for thinking of taking me. She opened my eyes to a world I had put aside.

Ultimately, she and my brother gave up their Washington Ballet tickets to me. That same year, I signed up for tickets to the Kennedy Center Ballet series. Now I go to the ballet frequently. Instead of becoming a prima ballerina, I have treated myself to the season's ticket series. I am finally learning about ballet by watching it. In fact, I am going to look into classes to teach myself more "appreciation" for the subject.

My point is, you never know where your joy will come from. You can turn a disappointment into a triumph if you will just look at it from a different angle. Not only do I go frequently to the theater to watch ballet performed professionally, but now two of my granddaughters are dancing seriously in their age groups. Their bodies must have inherited some flexibility genes I lack completely. I am so proud of them. I applaud their devotion to their classes and the art. The truth is, it is more fun to watch a ballerina than it probably is to be one. Those women work harder at their profession than most any other profession I can think of. Sometimes it may be that your dreams will work out in ways you never could have imagined by yourself.

My own personal belief is that we all are constantly aided by forces we do not understand. For me, the concept of a guardian angel has always been reassuring. Some people would say it was their Higher Power, or God, or an "inner guide" of some kind assisting them, but it is the same idea. We are not in this world alone.

You can be aided by this belief as you set out to accomplish your goals. I have a saying on a plaque on my office door that says: "Be Bold and Mighty Forces Will Come to Your Aid."

So let's get started, shall we?

WRITE A JOURNAL

To start, put down one or two things that you know you would like to do; then add from there. It is easy once you start. Starting is the hardest part.

I will wait. Go get a pen and paper right now while you are reading this. Do not hesitate. You may never get to it if you put it off even one more day.

Okay. Did you write down a couple of things? Please take this seriously. You cannot imagine the power of your own desires. We do not understand all the ramifications of thought and desire, but they are mighty. Do not dismiss them lightly. This is the key to achieving what you wish for. It will never happen without your focus and your will to further your own future. But we do this in all sorts of subtle ways. Perhaps you do it in dreams. Perhaps you draw sketches or string little thoughts together as you exercise.

I believe we polish our dreams daily without really knowing it.

Some people stop their dreams cold by negative thinking. Negative energy is powerful. Do not underestimate it. That is one of the reasons I advocate watching a happy DVD or reading a book that amuses you before bed and *never* watching the nightly network news before you sleep.

In my search for ideas and from listening to other women

in the second half of their lives, one thing pops up at me over and over. Women who have the happiest lives seem to actively believe in happiness. Other women simply expect disappointments and betrayals. And they receive them, just as expected. Expecting happiness may be a learned skill. Or, perhaps, some women do not have the mental flexibility to turn their negative thoughts off or redirect them. Just as I *never* could be a ballerina, it is possible that some women could never do what I am asking you to do.

Prove me wrong here, please.

I believe we all can do this, but it may be easier for some than others. Perhaps we choose who we are going to be in this life before we are born. Perhaps we need to suffer certain things in order to fulfill some other "Greater Plan." Of this, however, we can never be sure. I still believe it is best to try to be happier and more productive all of our lives. For me, it works consistently.

THE GIFT OF JOURNALING

Journaling helps you pick up on threads that may need to be picked out of the fabric of your life. Just as spreading a cloth out to look at the pattern will give you a better view of the whole, writing thoughts in a journal and then rereading it will make you an observer rather than just center stage in the dramas of your life. Once you are able to stand outside of yourself and your dramas, you can see more clearly and objectively what steps need to be taken. This is fun as well.

There are many approaches to writing a journal. I love the computer for journaling because of the ease of typing. Sometimes it seems I can type my thoughts as fast as I have them. When I used to write in diaries of paper with a pen, I constantly lost my train of thought, as my hands could not keep up with my brain.

But on the other hand, it is *most* satisfying to write the words with your own hand. To choose a book, a pen and the color of ink to use makes it an art form as satisfying as painting a painting or composing music. Creative work is creative. The more you do it, the broader will be your focus, or the narrower, if that is where you are heading.

Sometimes we need to dissect an action or a conversation or a dream. Sometimes we need to fly high above it and see things in the greater context. Either way, writing it down aids comprehension.

Here's another journaling activity: Examine the lives of others whom you admire. Make a list of people whom you want to know more about. Do some research. Find out if they have written books or if there are books written about them. Borrow some of these. Audio books are convenient and useful if you spend a lot of time in the car.

It inspires us to hear of the trials and tribulations that led our heroes to success in their field. Also, it helps to discover, as we all must, that their lives were full of human failings just like ours. Sometimes you discover that there are similarities and even pointers for action on your part in the stories of others.

Many times I have been inspired to seek a new avenue or a higher calling because of something I read in a book or was told in person by a mentor. Even movies help. When I was 11 years old, I saw the movie, *Desiree* (1954), which was made from the wonderful book of the same name by Annemarie Selinko. The heroine in the film, played by the actress Jean Simmons, wrote in a lovely diary. It was leather-bound, gold-tooled and filled with lovely, creamy blank pages. Watching her in the movie inspired me to do the same.

Up to that point in my life, I had used diaries with days listed numerically and pages lined. I was so inhibited that I tried to be sure my entries never went into the space for the next day. This distracted me, causing me to truncate thoughts and censor ideas due to lack of space. Thank God, I saw a more empowering example in the movie, after which I went right out and I bought myself an unlined diary. As a result, I began to keep more authentic records of my thoughts.

Even so, I still had such a fear of breaking the rules that whenever I *did* use a lined daily diary, I was afraid to write in information in the wrong day. What was I so afraid of? Why did I disown my own creativity in that way? I was only 12 or 13 when I saw the diary in the movie *Desiree*, but I felt that I was too old to change. I was worried about my old diaries that were written on a daily basis in small pages. It seems laughable to me now, but it was a serious worry back then.

I was 12 years old, and I feared I was too old to change. Don't let that happen to you. Change is the one certainty in life. Accept it and be glad that you can choose it, because sometimes it chooses you, and then you are forced to change when you least wish to.

I wonder how many people inhibit themselves with such wrong-headed reasoning. Just because you did something in error before does not mean you must continue doing that same thing wrong. Nor should you castigate yourself. Simply move on and do better in the future. This is true in *all* aspects of life.

As a child, I often kept some notes on people whom I admired. I wrote about the way they did things. If something they said or did or wore impressed me, it went directly into my diary of the moment. Keeping a list of people and ideas that you admire justifies the journal even if you are shy about writing your deepest thoughts in it.

If one author particularly inspires you, write to him or her. Many times this will lead you to unexpected friendships and new avenues to explore. My former husband carried on a long correspondence with the author Stephen Jay Gould before his untimely death. It all started with a letter that my former husband wrote to Gould about breeding Jack Russell terriers. Gould answered back and from that was born a friendship carried on entirely by letter. Years later, when we actually met Gould, we found him to be a very shy and uncommunicative in person.

For me, writing to and about someone I admire has worked in ways that are hard to imagine. I am writing this book indirectly because of a woman whom I admire immensely. The scientist and author Dr. Candace Pert first came to my attention in the '70s. She was written about in a magazine that I read as a young woman, and the article caught my eye. Over the years, I followed her career with interest. When she wrote her first book, *Molecules of Emotion,* years later, I bought it and went to a lecture she gave in Washington, DC. It was exciting to see her in person and meet her when she signed my book during a break in the lecture. We began to talk and found we had a lot in common.

I ultimately worked for her for a time, and though I have had several careers since then and several unfinished books, the writing of *Ahead of the Curve* is basically due to her in one way or another. Her friend and co-author, Nancy Marriott, coached me for a time while I began to write this book.

All of this stemmed from me taking the initiative to go to see Candace Pert in person. Of course, it also helped that I spoke up and brought our similarities to her attention. But my point is that you must follow your best instincts to seek out people you admire. Magic can happen, and often does.

It's Never Too Late

Have you thought about what you would like to accomplish in the next 50 years? What is left undone? Do you need a college degree? Do you want to change directions completely? What did you put off while working at a job you needed to keep during the years of children and mortgages? Perhaps it is time to come back to that. Or perhaps there is another way to approach it.

Just be sure that you never say it is *too late* to do anything. It may be too late to be a professional dancer, or a college basketball player, but it is not too late to watch them. Use your dreams to point yourself in the direction you wish to go. Then buy the tickets. Go to the performance. Read the books. Take action.

Do you crave travel? Try to find a way to gain access to a travel agency or a travel magazine or a cruise ship company. Sometimes just by volunteering you can learn where opportunities lie. Many opportunities show up when you teach a group of people something that you know but they do not. Many spas or cruise ships or vacation spots will give you free accommodations in return for your spending time teaching your skill to the guests. You may end up with a paying job or a way to be involved with the very thing you have always dreamed of doing but were afraid had passed you by.

It is not too late to learn more about a subject. In fact, you may have much more time than you think. Thinking in terms of many years makes it seem less audacious to go off on a tangent that your friends and family do not understand. Even though I am well past 50 now, I still think in terms of having 50 more years to live. And do you know what? I just might. Breakthroughs in medicine, memory enhancement and joint replacement may keep us healthy well into our hundreds.

Even if you don't make it to the end of what you start, who

knows what minor miracle you may work. And what a wonderful example you will be to millions of younger people who are still wandering around in the first 50 years of life.

MAKE A PLAN

Don't put it off another minute. Write out a plan for getting what you want. Even if some of it is not practical, write about it. This will help you clarify your desires. It will please you to write it down. It will show you where you need more information. Make a plan, an action plan. Set a time limit for getting what you want accomplished. The time limit becomes very important as you go along with your plan.

I have started many a book that still lies unfinished somewhere in my storage or even on this very computer that I am writing on now. Knowing this about myself, I decided to give myself a schedule to use to finish this book in a timely manner. In order to do that I hired a coach to help me get the book out on time. I cannot begin to tell you the huge difference this has made. For one thing, I feel guilty if I do not work on the book daily or at least most days. And I can see more progress because it does not languish for weeks unnoticed on my hard drive. It is a living, breathing thing now.

Writing a book is a lot like being pregnant. At first it is exciting and new; then it just becomes routine. Eventually, it has a life of its own and kicks and moves around, disturbing you when you are trying to sleep. It demands your attention even though it is still just a "work in progress"—the formation of ideas and not yet a finished product. Finally, it is formed, finished in its entirety. But there is still minor editing to do, and it seems to take forever. All the time the goal of birth seems so unattainable.

Will this *never* end?

Then one day it is time. The finished product is lying in your hands. You cannot believe it. What a triumph! The "unfinishable" is finished. Hurrah!!!

But it would never have happened without a plan. Believe me. I have tried writing books without one, and it does not happen. Happily, the planning idea works with everything. It works with completing school or online classes. It works with building muscles in your body, even when you've had reconstructive surgery. Whatever you want to do, you must write a plan for it first. My favorite early stage of planning is writing in a journal, but you may find a better way for yourself.

Whatever works is fine.

Just do it!!!

CHAPTER 2

WHAT LIFE? GET ONE!

I would rather regret the things I have done, than the things I haven't.

—LUCILLE BALL, ACTRESS

As Lucy knew so well, it's better to have lived and lost than never to have lived at all. The expression, *Get a Life*, reflects that sentiment. We think of life as something that comes at us, but a more enlightened view is that life is something we must create.

And seriously, you have to get a life in order to be ready for a relationship or find your next career, or be a good grandparent. Or simply to be content as you are right now. Begin by taking stock of what you have, your strengths, your talents, your blessings. From there, figure out what you think is missing. Be prepared to write it all down.

Here is the story of how I began to figure it all out for myself.

MADAME MARIE CURIE

A woman who influenced me with her success was the Nobel Prize winner, Madame Marie Curie. When I tell this to other women, many agree that she inspired them, too. Of course, the sad fact may be that there were not that many role models for my generation, leaving us with few choices.

Madame Curie lived in a time when women simply did not pursue careers that required intellect unless they were school teachers or nurses. Even women in those occupations were at a much-reduced status compared to men of their time. But Marie Curie was a scientist. She succeeded because she was simply so smart that she was able to transcend barriers in place at the time. Even so, she was thwarted often when it came to recognition. But she persevered and eventually received individual recognition. While she was married to a scientist of great ability, she was able to use her talents more or less under his name. Later, when he died, she continued with her work. She simply did what she had to because she was driven to go on.

She knew what she had to do, and she did it. I loved her story when I was young because of the romance, the tragedy of her husband's early death, and the fact that she did not let any of that stop her. But in her time, she could only do one thing at a time. She chose to continue her work. However, her personal life more or less stopped with widowhood. No one expected her to marry again. She threw herself into her work. She dressed as an older woman. She had no glamour. She wore mourning clothes and stayed to herself. (I hope that she found some romance and kept it hidden from the world.) However, I suspect that she kept the memory of her husband and his early death foremost in her thoughts.

It was fashionable in that age to consider one's love life finished with the death of a husband. Also, the anticipation of old age then was a different sort from that which we experience today. Old age started after 40. One just got more and more old. The styles worn by widows shouted their status. No one thought of dressing to connote joy. No woman in that age group would do what my mother advises and practices today: "A single woman must always sparkle!" That would have been shocking. It may be a bit shocking even now!

"SPARKLE!"

Years ago when I was still married and my mother was a widow, she told me, "A single woman must always sparkle." I thought that was amusing. She always seemed to be wearing jewels of some sort. She took a liking to sweaters decorated in jewels or spangles. Often I commented on her attire disparagingly, as only a daughter can.

But my mother liberated herself from widow's clothes. Today, in her 90s, she loves pastels, bright colors, anything except stark white or severe black. She also goes out all the time. She loves to dance.

Now, in the 21st century, Madame Curie would be out and about. She would be asked out to gatherings and included in many things simply because of her interest and ability. She could be dressed as a busy and successful scientist. Her clothes could be chic or rumpled, but they would be younger in style than the shapeless black frocks of her time. She could date. She could perhaps have found another scientist or a young lover to enjoy herself with. She would be able to live a full life today while a hundred years ago, it was positively shocking and upsetting that she continued on with her career. Rules had to be changed simply so that she could receive an award for her work.

Times have changed, thank goodness!

I ignore any disapproving glances and wear something sparkly every day, and so can you. You could wear red. You could sparkle. You choose.

But do not fade into the woodwork in drab unappealing clothes. Show yourself off. It is not your figure you are showing off, it is your wisdom. It is not your youth you are proudly exhibiting, but your age. Age is a banner. It is a thing to be treasured and sometimes even flaunted. Be proud that you have survived. Be aware of the gift of age and wisdom.

Shine. Enjoy. And give back to those who are younger and still not seasoned.

Be a beacon.

Be a role model.

THE GOOD FIGHT

We live today in an era where we are able to control our own lives and do pretty much as we wish. It is worth noting that this has not always been the case. Young women today often seem to forget that the previous generation fought to get where we are today. It is not just our "right," we earned it. Our grandmothers earned the vote with their efforts, at least my grandmother's generation did. In the '60s and '70s, when many of us baby-boomers were just starting out in life, Women's Liberation was nearly a bad word depending on whom you asked. Many women at that time spent their adult lives fighting to make it easier for their younger sisters today.

Now, in the early years of the 21st Century, we must fight our way to recognition once again. We must fight the invisibility that befalls women in their 50s and beyond. Just watch women in any big box store, like Best Buy. The sales clerks rush around waiting on absolutely everyone before deigning to help an older woman. They think we are not computer literate. They think we will not buy anything expensive. Do they think these women are just not worth the effort? Think again, young men. We are a force to be reckoned with.

However, not all of us fight. I see women all the time who look as if they have completely given up. This sort of grayed-out humanity is not specific to women, but we have a worse time of it. I know that many people who grew up in the '60s and '70s are proud of *not* conforming in dress and hairstyle. They pride themselves on being above the petty demands of fashion. Well, okay, but I hate to tell you that after 50 you must pay attention to your looks if you do not want to disappear completely. This seems so unfair. It appears to be gender-specific. Men can get away with looking totally out of style or disheveled and still be taken seriously. Women cannot.

No matter how successful you have been, you must remember to enter a new environment with the power light turned on. Your posture, your tidiness, your tone of voice and general attitude all dictate how well you will be treated. Perhaps you were beautiful when you were young. For you the change in attitude of others can be brutal. You must accept it and move into your inspired age with a different set of tools for being able to deal with the world.

If you refuse to do this, you will find that you lag behind others. I have watched this phenomenon for years. Women simply *must* rework their wardrobes. What will cause you to be seen as a viable target for the salesman? Wear clothes that fit. Add some color and perhaps something that flows or flutters about you.

You can wear a headband or a barrette that glitters. You can wear a sequined scarf, one of my favorite things to wear. You can wear a brilliant studded tee shirt or sweatshirt or blouse. Once I owned a black chenille sweater with a bright red spangled heart on the front. I wore it till it just fell apart. Where can I find another?

I have a handbag that I simply love. Its leather strap is decorated with brilliants that remind me of the decorations on my childhood cowboy (cowgirl, in my case) holster for my toy gun. Sometimes I wear a sparkly headband. I also own a shear, spangled scarf that I wear long, hanging down outside of my jackets. Sometimes I wear all of the above together!

At first I believed that the sparkling was only to attract men. However, now I see it as a way to stay in the line of vision of everyone we deal with in our daily lives.

Years ago, when I was a young bride, the activist and author Betty Friedan wrote her book, *The Feminine Mystique*. It was a book that profoundly disturbed the status quo. She shook the tree. She changed thinking for a whole generation of women. Many women of that time had never even thought of themselves as "victims," but were. They went about things in the way they had been told to by their mothers and by the popular magazines that they read. Movies supported the old model. There were no Internet *blogs* to use to discuss dissatisfaction. Women were often silent prisoners. They had no independent incomes. They were basically helpless without their husbands. Betty Friedan opened their eyes. She made them think about their lives and their choices.

And that's what I intend to do. I want to change the way older women think. The best way to change anything is simply to do it yourself and let others find you and ask what you did. I cannot wait. Too many women think their lives will be over after 50.

65 IS THE NEW 40

Think again! Things have changed. I read somewhere that 65 is the new 40. I loved that phrase because it is even more radical a statement than I would have made. But there is truth in it. For example, when your mother was 40-45, she had the energy status and sex appeal of women who are now in their 60s. Look at Meryl Streep and the woman she portrays in *Mama Mia*. Something truly revolutionary has happened to aging. I want to help this new movement along as much as I am able.

Deepak Chopra said on *Larry King Live* that the fastest growing segment of the population is the centenarians! That's another revolutionary thought.

I believe that Willard Scott, my friend and television personality, the wonderful Weatherman from NBC News, is partially responsible for this revolutionary idea. Willard is a neighbor of mine in the Virginia countryside. He was so much a part of the general landscape of my early years. He has lived much of the time near the tiny village of Paris, Virginia. His daughters went to school with mine. I see him from time to time socially. So I have been able to ask him personally about his views on this subject. Naturally, he made the whole thing into a joke. Right up to the present, he is making people laugh on morning television.

Willard used to begin his broadcasts with a birthday wish for some "little old lady" who had just reached her 100th birthday. He told me that they added that segment to the show in 1984. At first, about once a week, he would hold up a picture of some wizened old woman and wish her a Happy Birthday. But then something unexpected happened. More and more women were writing to say that their birthdays were coming up. Many of them were over 100! The picture of a wizened old lady was replaced with smiling attractive women who looked as if they not only had all their marbles, but also could blow out the candles on their cakes without any help—and dance on their birthdays!

Willard told me that they had to stop reading about *each*

woman, because they received so many cards that it would have taken up the entire show. No one would have known what the weather was going to be, he quipped. So many women wrote in because they were proud of their great age. In fact, more and more of them were over 100 years old.

As a woman, I have to believe that many of those women began to be a little bit competitive about how long they would live. If one older woman had reached her 100th birthday, her friends who saw her name and picture on Willard Scott's program wanted to make it, too. As other women in other areas began to understand how many women were living to 100 (and even more), they adjusted their own thinking and decided they wanted to go on as well. Because of Willard Scott's showcasing women who had reached 100 years, he gave hope to thousands of women who determined to reach that goal as well.

Of course, this is only my own theory. It is not scientific; I cannot prove it. But other women will understand the feminine rivalry that is related to the way women compete with each other in areas of beauty or brains. We love our sisters, but we enjoy outliving them, too.

So, believe you can live to be 100. Believe you will be healthy while you live. Believe you will find a man with whom you will be happy, if that is what fits your dream. Believe it, and take some time to actually decide what you want. Oh, and don't forget: *Write it down!*

THE FOUR-MINUTE MILE

I love to tell people about the story of the four-minute mile. When I was a young girl, people said that the mile could never be run in four minutes, let alone less. But one day in May 1954, the record was broken by Roger Bannister (later Sir Roger Bannister), His record did not last very long. Soon the four-minute mile was broken again, and again, and again—16 times by 1957.

Part of the reason, perhaps all of the reason, it was not broken before was because the idea had taken hold that there was a physical limitation on human beings that precluded running this fast. It was a physical barrier in the mind only. There was no truth to it, but it held men back nevertheless. Once other runners knew it could be broken, they adjusted their thinking to allow for the possibility that they, too, could break the record.

Half of getting a job done is imagining it done. Believing you will do something makes it much more likely that you will. When we accomplish something that seemed impossible to others, it gives us the confidence to do more because we believe we can. In fact, I am not sure you can do anything that you don't believe you can, at least subconsciously. And it may be that it must be a conscious thought in order for it to work. It is all about intention and the belief that you are capable of accomplishing something that is not the norm, or perhaps something that has never been done before.

I love to see the fuse get lit. It gives me such pleasure to see women come out of their shells and begin to participate in life. They never thought they could, but they did, and they are.

What you don't know, you don't know. Think about that. It is really quite profound. We all have an area of knowledge that is not accessible to our conscious mind. This hidden cache contains all that our blind spots prevent us from seeing and understanding. That knowledge may be hidden, but it is very possibly there in code, undecipherable in its present form. Allow for this! Look deeply inside. Hunt and dig and find what else is in there. You may find the ability or grit or perseverance that you were unaware of on a conscious level.

We, all of us, are so powerful. All of us contain hidden

strengths. All of us need a push of some kind to discover them. Read self help books. There are so many, it may be difficult to choose. May I suggest my favorites? One of the absolute top authors of self-improving and thought-provoking books is Robert Allen. Also Brian Tracy, Joe Vitale, Louise Hay, Anthony Robbins, or Eckhart Tolle. All of these have been an unbelievable influence on my life. It is hard to choose a few when there are so many competent inspirational speakers and writers to study. For the *very* dedicated, there is *A Course in Miracles*. The *Course* cannot be done easily or quickly, but it can change your life. This can become addictive. It feels good to learn about your hidden depth.

Keep at it.

Abigail Trafford specializes in helping women understand and deal with divorce. Her books have given solace and practical advice to countless women struggling with various problems related to finding themselves suddenly single.

Chapter 3

Where Are the Men?

The opinion of 10,000 men is of no value if none of them know anything about the subject.

—Marcus Aurelius, Roman Orator

You think there are no men out there?

They say there are *NO* women! So be careful when you say they aren't there—because they are.

They just may not be where you expect to see them.

Truth is there are many men out there, men of all age ranges and preferences in women. Some are not "out there" in the dating marketplace, but rather sitting at home—alone and lonely. Many have opted out of showing up at the usual spots, having become discouraged by the desperate attempts so many women make to get their attention. Many others simply reiterate, "There are just no decent women out there, so why bother?" By *decent* they do not mean chaste. They mean attractive and energetic, non-complaining and cheerful women.

So be one of those women.

FIND THOSE MEN

If you're alive, you can date. And you can find available men. Here's how to do it: Make a list of all the men you know. *All* of the single men, including doctors, policemen, bums, teachers, mechanics, co-workers. You may surprise yourself with just how many single men you know.

You may have to ask some of them, "Are you single?" But there is no harm in doing this. Many men will be only too happy to tell you the details about how they got that way, or why they have never married—especially if you learn to speak in a friendly, non-threatening way when you are asking a man a personal question. It's a great opportunity to practice on men whom you are *not* interested in. Then, when you are faced with a man who makes your heart pound, you will be able to speak to him without losing control completely and feeling embarrassed or inexperienced.

I keep a running list of available men. I add to it every time I come across someone new. Sometimes it is sad how the list keeps changing. Men die. Men get married. And men become too old to participate in the male/female social interaction we have been speaking of. Sickness claims some. However, most men, no matter how old or sick, like to have female companionship. Be a friend to a sick man and you may meet a healthy friend who comes to visit. Niceness is rewarded in proportion to its sincerity. The Golden Rule works no matter what you are doing. Never let it be forgotten.

My list keeps growing because I find new men everywhere. I ran into one at an informal dinner at a restaurant when someone asked me to join their table. Someone who works for me part time told me about one of her other employers. She said that he says, "There are no decent women to be found." Now that I know about him, I shall add his name to my list of single men and invite him to a party. I bet I'll have him paired off by the end of the year.

Pairing off of single men with women eats most heavily into my list of men. Men love to pair up. They need someone to take care of them. We women really do not. It is human to want a partner, and it follows that after we recover from any psychic wounds left from a break up, we become receptive once again to the man who is, in return, receptive to us.

But it is more likely that the newly single man will find a partner quickly, than for you. That is because men who have been in a partnership know they like having someone to take care of them, and they want another one, quickly. In the meantime, women function very well by themselves. They are not lonely because they have women friends to bond with. Also, women are more selective as a rule, leading to the impression that "there are *no* men out there," while many men appear to fix on the very first woman who smiles at them, works with them, or flirts with them at a gathering. So they seem to be "taken" sooner than many single women.

However, if a man isn't married, he is still a single man, regardless of his being taken or not. It is not as if we were trying to break up long standing couples. Often, newly single men are still not certain of the length of time they want to be with a woman and may just be using her as a "place holder" until a more ideal woman comes along. Be careful in these situations. You want to avoid falling unaware into being a placeholder for anyone. Choose a man who really wants *you*, not someone who just wants a bedtime story. Unless that's all that you want.

Men are not exactly in hiding, but rather do often prefer to stay by themselves. They do not feel the same desire to go out that women do. They are happy alone in front of the TV and often prefer it to a noisy bar. Some are just happy sitting with their favorite dog in front of a warm fire. Given this is so, you must train yourself to be alert and intentional. You need to listen when people are speaking of a local widower or divorced man. You need to write down names and places. These important facts will escape you later, so write them down every time you hear them.

Next, write down a list of single women. They know where many of the men are. Your women friends will often be the ones who help you find a new friend and lover. Other times, they are jealous of single women and not helpful at all. Try to find women who are interested in helping their "sisters" and who have the confidence to know that they will be all right by themselves, even if you find a man first. In fact, what you want is the friendship of women who are content as they are. And that is who you want to be, too. A "happily single" status will make you a lot more attractive when you do meet a man. They hate it when we appear needy and desperate.

BE WHERE THEY ARE

Once you have sharpened your awareness and have let go of your negative expectations, become even more proactive. There are several things you can do to position yourself more positively to meet men.

For one, plan to take up at least one sport or hobby that is more "man-oriented" than "woman-oriented." Not to be sexist here, but there are some sports that men enjoy engaging in more than do women. What do you enjoy doing for sport? Are you a tennis player? Does golf intrigue you? Do you play cards? Bridge and poker are very popular games. Taking up a sport is good for you. This will allow you to keep both your mind and body sharp, also. If you do not play a sport, then perhaps you prefer to watch others. Do you have tickets for games, or do you know someone who does? What is the most likely place where you meet a man whom you want to see again? Could you find him in the food line at a football game? Or will you take golf lessons *from* him?

Do you like to travel? There are many, many different types of trips you can take. They range from inexpensive to expensive. Broaden your horizons by going to see places where you have never been. There are a multitude of stories about women meeting men on cruises, on walking tours, and at wine tours overseas. Meet new people, both on the trip and in groups, and be sure to recall the details for conversation later. You will be more interesting to a new man you are meeting if you have something to tell about a recent trip. Stick to discussions about subjects that men will also enjoy. Forego the garden club tour in favor of an archeological dig or an adventure type of cruise.

Do you stay only with women, all the while moaning about the fact that there are no men around? Go where the men are.

Ask everyone you know to introduce you to someone you do not know—of any age or sex. This leads to more and more acquaintances and, therefore, greater chances of finding just the right person for you. In the meantime, enjoy it—the sport, the new hobby, the trip, and meeting new people.

The Party Plan

When I was newly single, part of my original plan to "stay in the running" and avoid becoming marginalized was to have two parties at my house every month. Some people gasp when I say this. They think that it sounds difficult or expensive. For me it is neither.

Intellectually I knew that as soon as I separated myself from my husband of 42 years, I would drop out of sight if I did not take measures to prevent that. I have always found it fun to give parties. When I was younger, they were more formal and well thought out. They were actually time-consuming and difficult to arrange and give.

When I began to entertain as a single woman, I readjusted my thinking. Finally I realized that it is the people who make a party. Get a good group of people together, and they will be their own party. Feed them well but simply, oil the evening with wine and cool drinks, and the festive gathering will all come together by itself.

So. I made a promise to myself to have two parties every month. For the first two years, I never missed a single month from the day my ex-husband and I separated. I have already told the story of that day when I bought three bunches of roses and invited some friends over for drinks. I had fun and thoroughly enjoyed myself. I bet there are not many women who can say that on the first day of separation! But not only did I have fun, I felt free. I knew I was free to invite anyone I wanted, even people whom my former spouse might not have wanted to see or invite.

I no longer have so many parties, but it certainly served its purpose. I did not simply disappear socially. By expanding my acquaintances, I have changed my life a lot. I now have a list of 50 single men and just as many single women. I only have one party a year that is exclusively for single people, and that is my Valentine's Day dinner party.

All of my other parties include men and women who are couples, either married or simply "couples without wedding rings." I sprinkle in plenty of singles, too. I invite many more single people now than I would have if I were not single myself. It is really important to keep your name on the lips and in the memory of your friends and new acquaintances. You never know what this may lead to. But if you are forgotten, you will never have the chance to discover your new loves and to make new friends.

This is *all* entirely up to you. So please do not complain if you feel left out. You can change your situation if you will lift your hand to help yourself.

THE INTERNET

The Internet is a safe way to expand your social and romantic reach. I believe in Internet dating. It works. Sometimes the results are surprising in their speed, and then some of these "meetings" are a waste of time. Getting quick results are gratifying if you are impatient, but they are often only a quick fix. On the other hand, it is slow sometimes, but it does eventually lead to meeting men you would *never* have met any other way.

If you look at the ads put online by men, you will begin to understand that there are just as many of them looking for us as there are women looking for them.

For one thing, not all women are looking for a man. Many are content to be alone. Or maybe some of them are just wounded or cynical, or simply tired of kissing "frogs." Never mind! It is fine that at any given time there are many women who are not interested. That just makes it easier for *you*.

Men, on the other hand, are often looking for someone who is *not* you. Many of them are hung up on the idea of a younger woman. Many of them are gay. I believe that being able to be out of the closet has definitely shrunk the supply of men. But do you really want a man who is gay but scared to admit it? No, of course not. So just be glad that you don't have to worry too much about this. It does not hurt to be slightly suspicious about their sexual orientation, though. Bi-sexual men are more likely to carry the HIV virus. Any man—gay or hetero—could be a carrier, and we simply have to be careful of all STDs. Don't be

afraid to ask. And don't be afraid to ask for proof. It is dangerous to just assume.

My original personal favorite is *Match.com*, because it is
just so easy to use. *Yahoo Personals* is also good. Then there are
a myriad of knockoffs, some better than others. *EHarmony* is
good for the very timid. It keeps so many layers of safety between you and any potential man that you must be truly dili-
gent to get to the real person.

Perhaps your college or university has a matching site. Or
you can find sites for different age groups: over 30, over 40,
over 50 and so forth. I think it is best *not* to limit yourself to
an age too close to your own. You are free now to go outside
the old norm. You are not a 20-year-old with no knowledge of
the world. Use your wisdom and experience to keep you safe as
you explore online dating sites that are focused on personality,
not age. And just to prove I really mean that, there is *www.Go-
Cougar.com,* which is a site where older women can find much
younger men. And you would be surprised how many younger
men seem to be attracted to older women.

TAKE UP A SPORT

Golf is a great sport to take up for meeting men. I myself
plan to take up golf because it is fun and allows you to have
something active to do almost anywhere you go. A woman
friend of mine who has played golf for years told me to find a
friend who wants to learn, too. Then I must make a plan with
her to play every week. Lessons are a must. But without actually
playing with someone around the entire course, I know I will
never progress to the level I wish to be. So I must make a plan
to go play golf.

What I want is to be good enough for it to be fun to play
with a mixed foursome. Because of handicaps, it is possible for

a lesser golfer to play with good ones, but you do want to be confident about your game, even if it is still not a great one. So practice first with a friend.

MALE INTERESTS

Stocks and bonds are a fascination with many men. Go to conferences and seminars about trading. The ratio of men to women is staggeringly in your favor. Besides that, you may learn something to make you money.

It always makes sense to do something you actually like to do. Otherwise you may go to something—some event, conference or discussion—that is simply out of the range of your normal likes and dislikes, and find a man there who wants to keep doing that thing and expects you to do it, too. Never pretend to be someone you are not. It leads to all sorts of problems, not the least of which is that you will never be happy.

LIGHTEN UP AND BE YOURSELF

Don't be judgmental. You do not know everything. You are single. You need to be forgiving of others' flaws and try to correct your own. You must not have too rigid a plan about meeting a new man. Life is rarely linear. Things rarely go in a straight line.

You will meet a man who is marvelously handsome but married. You will meet a man who interests you more than any other, yet is of a different race or religion. Do not write him off. You are grown up now. You are probably not going to have any more children. Your parents are most likely elderly or gone. Please yourself. Perhaps it is time to step over the traces and do something completely unlike yourself. You may be amazed at the results.

The important thing to remember here also is: *be yourself.*

Do not try to mold yourself to someone who is so different that you lose your true self. Of course, this is easier said than done if you fall head-over-heels in love with someone. Even though you now have a great deal of wisdom due to having lived through so much and having seen so much, you must still have the discipline to act on that wisdom.

DRAWING YOUR LINE

You must realize for yourself what you are willing to live with, and what you are *not*. You may be a sportswoman but fall in love with a couch potato.

Does this ever happen? Yes, it does. What's important is that you know where to draw your line.

You may be a rollicking, sexy, juicy woman who wishes to express your love physically to your man. But your man may have a Madonna/whore complex—where the woman who is his mate seems to be too pure to sully with sexual congress—and be unable to make love to you.

What do you do in such a case? Well, that depends on what is most important to you. If you love other things about that man, perhaps you can sublimate your sexual drive. Just be careful. If you are not excruciatingly honest with yourself, then you are doomed to failure. And if you are honest with yourself, you had better be honest with him, too.

So often, the sexual drive of a man and a woman are not in synch. This can be a real problem. However, if you will speak to each other without blame or accusations, there can often be a compromise that pleases both parties. If things really are unequal, you may need professional help. What one person sees as normal may come across as a perversion to their partner. Guilt and inhibitions from one's past can create insurmountable barriers to one's sex life.

Everyone wants to have a wonderful relationship with their lover. This can mean many different things to different people. There is no "normal." Whatever works for you as a couple is okay. Please do not agonize over your sexual needs. Enjoy them.

What if the man you choose and who chooses you turns out to have an addiction to some substance? Can you deal with that? I hope you will walk away right away, before you get totally destroyed by trying to love a drunk or drug addict. After he has beaten his addiction, that is the time to have this type of man. Once he has come to grips with his habit and found a spiritual anchor, he will be a much better mate. In fact, I recommend AA meetings as a place to meet men. But pick the ones who have been in the program for many years over a newcomer.

If you are an intellectual, can you settle for a man who simply reads the newspaper, or worse yet, finds the television all the source of news and information that he needs. Never opening a book could be a problem in a man who is married or living with a woman who wishes to discuss ideas, philosophies and perceptions. Can you do it? That depends. How long can you do it? That is a separate question.

Of course, in later life we do not have to speak of "forever" when we speak of relationships. It is really just fine to have more than one. The ideas that applied when we were young and looking for "lifelong" mates simply do not matter. We have already given up that philosophy by being single now. So let it go for the future, too. Perhaps you *will* find a mate forever. But if you just enjoy someone for a season, that may be just right for you.

FINDING THE ONE

Thank goodness there isn't just one--The One. There need to be many "The Ones," all of whom could be Mr. Right, because by the time you have lived enough years to be in the second half of life, you may have already gone through more than one of the Mr. Rights of your acquaintance. There are still more out there. Don't give up. Don't *ever* give up.

The fact is that the many possible men are still few and far between. It may be years and years before that man who is just right for you comes into your life. You must accept this and relax. In fact, relaxing is a skill that all of us should learn. So often we try to force things to fit our view. Often that includes men who are hopelessly wrong for us.

When you think about it, there is good reason that it is so hard to find just the right person. It is meant to be difficult, rare. What if we found just the type of man that we wanted once a month? Once we have picked one, it would be very awkward to then find another one the very next month. No one would ever be safe. Even after settling on one man, you would be tempted all the time by others. There is a good reason to wait and find a man who is just right for *you*. This may take time. And, of course, I guess the pessimists among you will say that it could just never happen. That could be true. But it is not likely. I believe there is more than one "The One" for everyone.

Don't be discouraged, even if it has been five years and you still have not met the right one. It doesn't matter. Wait for the right one. Be patient. Relax and have some fun along the way. Don't disappear into a hole. Stay out in the open where you will be noticed by exactly the right man. Just remember that it may not happen the first time out of the gate.

Have you written down your description of your ideal man? If not, why not?

Don't you believe me? I mean it. Write it down. You cannot complain about not finding a super guy if you have not taken the time to put your request out there to the Universe.

One woman whom I interviewed was moving to another

state to live near her grown child. She went to look at a house to rent and discovered that it was a basement apartment instead. She spoke with the owner and said, "I don't want to rent your apartment, but I love your house and would love to live in it, instead." The man asked her out to dinner.

She has been happily married to him for ten years now.

SHIFT YOUR EXPECTATIONS

After my separation, I had to shift my expectations. I thought I would always be married. The divorce was shocking to our children and our family and friends. But I had to learn to take their reaction in stride. To go from being a solid couple to being a single is a jarring change in status. I had to learn to relax around others in my new "character" and enjoy myself as a single entity. The newness of it made it seem difficult.

At first, when you are separated after having been in a long-term relationship, you tend to be anxious. But you can force yourself to relax. The whole world is not talking behind your back. Nothing horrible is happening in their minds when you come into view. In fact, they are probably not thinking of you at all. After a while, you realize that your relaxation is natural. You are happy alone.

When my former spouse and I first told people we were separating, they wanted to know why. It was so tempting to try to explain it, even though it was simply *not* explainable to most people. Many people would have been more comfortable if I had said that my husband ran off with another woman, than that we both came to the end of our marriage. I suppose the fact that he did actually turn up with a younger woman who was blonde, mind you, may have made some of them feel that they understood what happened. But there is no way that they could see why our marriage just sort of gave out.

I like to say we ran out of energy. It was so important to me to have a loving relationship that I often went to extraordinary lengths to insure it stayed that way. It took a lot of effort and often included giving up things I wanted to do. I am sure that was also true for my husband. We both tried to keep it up. I used to work to make it appear easy, because it was what I wanted. As I aged and grew wiser and more independent, I understood that there was more to my life than my marriage. Each couple has their own level of resistance to the idea of divorce. Our marriage counselor told us we had "a better marriage than many" of her clients. That may be true, but for us it was over and with no regrets.

It was hard to be alone at first because I simply never had been alone. I was so used to being surrounded by people. Silence was a surprise. And I welcomed it. There were many times when I really loved the silence of the new, empty house. Nevertheless, I did fill it up with music when I could remember to turn on a CD player. Sometimes I simply never thought of it. I am not a television addict. In fact I just never turn it on except to play DVDs. That was my opiate, if I had one.

I spent a lot of time watching funny DVDs on evenings when I was not otherwise occupied with friends, parties, events or family. I wanted to make sure I *never* sat home feeling sorry for myself. Funny shows made me laugh. Sometimes I was simply howling with laughter—just me and my dog! It may sound sort of sad, but I did not feel that way. I felt like a child let loose from restrictive parents or school. I would *never* have been able to be so self-indulgent while married. I would never have been able to watch *Love, Actually* or *Moonstruck* twice in a row, just because those films gave me a warm glow.

DON'T LOSE HOPE

I want to give you all a feeling of hope. Just because you haven't met anyone doesn't mean there isn't anyone. The danger is that women settle for someone that they don't really love because they are expecting The One and get discouraged. They don't allow for the adventure, the experimenting. They get tired of expecting The One. This is a trap, the trap of The One and Only. For older women, it's worse. They remember that when they were teenagers, after a break-up they always found someone right away. Older women may feel the days rushing by. Time seems to go faster. So don't worry if the time gaps are longer. Even if there are many years in between, you still have plenty of time.

My mother married for the second time at age 81. When one looks at her wedding pictures, one is struck by her beauty. She was radiant and happy. Like a bride half a century younger, she simply glowed! Yet before she and her second spouse met, she thought she was finished with romance. She had sort of put that part of herself on a shelf. She had packed her sensuality away in a lavender tissue of age with sachets of memory to hold the scent of happiness. She felt she had had a lifetime of love already. But one day, after his wife died, the man that she loved when she was 17 called her up and asked her to go to dinner and a movie. They fell instantly back into the love they had so very many years before.

They were never apart after that dinner. The story is almost too romantic to believe. But I watched it unfold. I sat next to him at dinner one night sometime after they reconnected, and he said to me, "All I want to do with the rest of my life is make your mother happy."

How can you fault a man who will admit that? And it seemed

to be completely true. He never tired of her. They had only six and a half years together before he died, but those were the happiest years of my mother's life. She was 84 when he died.

My passion at this time in my life is to convince women it's okay to relax and feel hopeful. Rather than unhopeful and despondent, they have every right to assume something wonderful is right around the corner. Why not?

It is so important to understand that it is all a process. You cannot jump into a new relationship just because you feel lonely. You must enjoy the life you have. Find happiness in unexpected places. Give of yourself to people who are less fortunate.

The problem with older women is that they lose hope. They say, "Oh, it's too late for me." Or they criticize every man who is not "right" for them and say, there are *no* men out there. Then it becomes a self-fulfilling prophecy. How I hate to hear those words: "There are no men!"

BE AN ADVENTURESS

That is what I am proudest of: in the second half of my life, I've become an adventuress. In my first 50 years, I was much more conventional. Never did it occur to me to investigate younger men as a possibility, for instance. Going outside my race or religion seemed unwise when I was planning a family, even foolhardy. But now it makes no difference. In fact, it is a broadening adventure to grow close to someone who believes all sorts of different things and yet who loves you.

Be an adventuress. "Be bold, and mighty forces will come to your aid," wrote the famous German poet/playwrite Goethe almost two centuries ago. I love that quote. It is so true. But it is also very difficult to do when you are scared and alone and no longer young and beautiful, nor even thin anymore. Still, you must try.

Nothing will happen if you don't make it happen. Actually, the Universe is so capricious that sometimes things do actually happen right out of the blue. Even so, most of the time you must row your own boat.

So join clubs, go to religious services, not just church but church-sponsored activities. Go to events that are interactive, like auctions or dance contests or beach activities. If you can afford it, go on a cruise. That way, even if you do not meet anyone, you will be having a wonderful time anyway.

Look in the newspaper and discover what free events are happening on the weekend. Go to rallies and concerts and games in the park. As I said earlier, you need to go where the men are. Do not waste your time joining the Red Hat ladies except just to have fun on an off night. You will not meet men there. Go to car races, or horse races, or football games or sometimes just go to the market when men will be there. This is often at 6 pm on a Friday night. Or you might try going to get ice cream late at night. They do that, too.

Join marathon walking groups. Learn to go whitewater rafting or paddle a canoe or a kayak. Join a hiking club. Or join a group of bicyclers. Just be sure there are men as well as women in the group.

The point is *to connect*. One connection leads to another. And another and another. Before long, you will be too busy with all your activities. When that happens, you will have the delightful pleasure of choosing among your many activities. How amazing that will be.

Enjoy your success.

Chapter 4

Get Sexy

A figure with curves always offers a lot of
interesting angles.
—Wesley Ruggles, American Film Director

Oh, yes you can!!!
You are a woman. You *are* sexy!
Know it.
Feel it. Look for it.
First, look at your naked body. Learn to appreciate the parts of you that work. Surely there is a part of you that you really like. Perhaps your eyes sparkle. Perhaps they are large and expressive. Perhaps your have super breasts. Maybe your legs are statuesque. Are you tall? Some men are turned on by that. Are you short? There are many short men who are desperate to find a woman who does not tower above them.

Look at the front of yourself and the back. Notice how you look from the sides. Find something you can appreciate about your body. Begin to see yourself through the eyes of an appreciative male.

IT's ALL IN THE HEAD

There are so many types of men. Some prefer women who have the figures of models. That is true. But there are others who are really turned on by older women. Some men have a fixation with women old enough to be their mothers or more. You may be surprised to discover that men often find large women attractive. Some men are turned on by heavier women—heavier than that model-size figure. Some men just like a woman with curves. More curves are better than fewer curves to certain men. Men like women to feel soft and pliable when they put their arms around them. They do not like to be stuck in the ribs by a bony elbow.

Then there are the men who like Big Beautiful Women— *BBWs*. They actually *like* a large and corpulent woman. So, relax and trust that your body can be appreciated, even if you do not have the perfect figure.

Again, you can find what you need on the Internet. There are sites specifically for BBWs. Go there and lurk on a message board of a chat room. You will soon be validated. It is a revelation to some women that they are indeed sexy in spite of weight issues.

Many women who are lovely according to the latest fashion magazine are *not* sexy. Sexy is in your mind, not your figure. Many men have complained that they found a woman who was truly lovely but simply didn't care for physical intimacy. Mature men learn this lesson and remember it.

Not all men are able to reach past the image of the perfect woman. So if you find that sort of man becoming close to you but constantly needling you about what you eat, leave. If a man gives clues that he disrespects you due to a disconnect in his idea of what is beautiful and desirable, leave. It will do your self confidence *no good* to stay with such a man. Escape before you find that you start to believe him. Remember that.

You should already know by now that sex is about 90% in one's head. (It's been said that the brain is the largest sex organ.) That means the guy's head as well as yours. Attitude—about yourself, about your partner, about a potential relationship—is appeal! He is the one who will decide if you turn him on. Don't worry about it.

At the same time know that you are able to be sexy or *not* sexy—to feel it, to act it—depending on where your head is at the time. You can entice a man or drive him away. You can excite or dampen spirits. You can invite advances or restrict them simply by the way your body language translates to a man. And you can sometimes give the wrong idea by accident. Men read signals into all sorts of things that we do not even notice. But on the other hand, we judge them for things they had no idea that they were doing. It is a strange world—often a world of mixed messages between the sexes. In truth, it is hard to believe we *ever* get together, because our perceptions of each other are so very different.

JUST BE SEXY

Check out your wardrobe. If you do not have a few outfits that are suggestive, that make you feel alluring, buy something that is. Look at *Victoria's Secret* catalogues or *Frederick's of Hollywood*. They may inspire you to order something just for yourself. If you are large in size, order something that will fit you. These catalogues know that Big Beautiful Women are sexy, too.

They are often very accommodating for the larger figure. Find a catalogue like this for you.

Read about, watch movies about and talk about sex.

Feeling sexy is contagious. Yes, go ahead and *be* sexy. It is *okay* now. Read about sex. Rent movies that are hot and sexy. Write down your fantasies—romantic, sexy, and otherwise. Many of us do not even know what our fantasies are. We are afraid of making them concrete by truly imagining them. However, that is exactly what you need to do.

To help your imagination, read erotic literature. Words are nourishment for the soul as well as the mind. Open yourself to a huge array of possibilities.

Do not stay in a rut or a corner. Venture out of your comfort zone. Press the contours of your personal fear envelope. Push out, be brave and do not draw away at the first sign of pain or embarrassment.

Things happen. Sometimes you overstep. Some people misunderstand an overture and overreact. Do not become distracted. Finish what you start. Forge ahead even into the unknown and unknowable future. It may be longer and brighter than you ever could have imagined.

Do not limit your horizons with preconceived notions. Your horizons are vast, and you cannot possibly see the entire expanse from where you stand now. You must advance blind sometimes. I love the quote that I read somewhere that says: "Faith is walking to the edge of all the light you have and taking one more step."

Guts matter. Bravery will become second nature. Press on. Learn to push past fear and find the power that comes with facing your fears. Eleanor Roosevelt said, "You must do the thing you fear the most." Or something to that effect. Be sure that Eleanor probably was not referring to increasing your reach, sexually speaking, but she would be proud of you anyway. You have so much to offer. Offer it and be proud. Do not think that your life is over just because you are over 50 or 60 or 70 or more.

I had lunch with a beautiful woman whose figure was that of a girl. She said she felt that her time was past. I exclaimed with feeling, "You are at your peak!" I could see the surprise in her eyes. But it was true.

In the 21st century, the old rules simply do not apply. Remember: *65 is the new 40.* And if you look at the *young* women of 40 who are just entering into marriage and perhaps beginning to think about motherhood, you will know that this is true. Sixty-five is just a jumping off point for your sexual life. If you are single, the world is your oyster. The possibilities are endless. Men are just clamoring to be with you. Younger men find you amazingly sexy.

Go for it.

EXPAND YOUR HORIZONS

Take a trip. Meet someone online who is from another area of the world. There are many safe ways to do this. The important thing here is: Take action! It is so easy to procrastinate and make up all sorts of excuses about why you cannot do something. I have heard them all, because I have used them all.

Get scared. It is a sign that you are alive. Find new limits that will encompass your old ones, but give them plenty of room to grow. Keep an open mind. The world is changing so fast. You cannot keep up if you are stuck in old thinking. It is essential to push past your doubts and past your fears, as I have already said. Push the edge of the envelope when it comes to expanding your experiences.

Once upon a time, you had to travel physically to discover

what others were like and what a new culture might encompass. Now the Internet makes "virtual travel" a thing that is truly possible. If you concentrate on one area or country or new culture and decide to discover it, you will be blown away by the extent to which you can visit it online. Try it. Pick a city that has some object or building or past culture that you admire or want to know more about. Plug it into *Google* and start following links. You will find that there are not enough hours in the day to explore all that is available to you on the subject. It is a great adventure to see what you can see by simply plugging words in a search engine.

Similarly, I urge you again not to hesitate to explore the vast range of online dating sites. Use caution, of course, just don't be afraid to start. If you never start, you will never discover the secrets of the Internet when it comes to men and women. There is *no* better way to expand your horizons for meeting men.

If you simply look on a search engine for "dating" or "singles" or "meeting men," you will find a number of sites where you can begin your search. There is the ever-popular *Match.com*, as well as the super safe *eHarmony.com*. There are sites for specific schools so check your alma mater. There are sites for different age groups. Every sort of kinkiness is available, if that is what you seek.

One of the most interesting ideas is specific to younger men seeking older women. I mentioned *GoCougar.com* in the previous chapter. The cougar phenomenon is an old story in modern clothing. Many men have a deep-seated craving to be with older women. This can be fun for both. Older women are much more likely to be comfortable with their sexuality. They are not likely to seek a father for their unborn children. They are less likely to need marriage to complete them. So the men can relax. Everyone benefits.

One reason that I recommend starting online is the anonymity. You can make a fool of yourself without any serious repercussions. You can practice with false names. Just remember that if you are using a false identity, so might that man you meet online. Be cautious. Be aware. Be willing to have fun, and do not take it too seriously. You can reinvent yourself. Of course, I hope that what you ultimately do is find your true self.

The sexual self that lies waiting to be awakened by a man you have not yet met will emerge with practice. You need to know that it works. So try it. Don't be discouraged if some of the men turn out to be charlatans and liars. That is not solely the province of the Internet. Men and women, too, can sometimes be too self-conscious and insecure to tell the truth. Some of them feel that the simple truth would not be attractive.

Even young men feel this way. I used to know a man who would reserve a table in a restaurant saying that he was "Dr." so and so. He felt that he would receive better service and be more likely to be given a good table if he had a title depicting education of some kind. Sad but true, he was not confident enough of his own ability to elicit respect.

What you need to know is that you do not need a title or an education to be well thought of. And you do not need anything artificial to be sexy. Sexiness comes from confidence in one's self. It is a mindset. You will never get it out of a book, though.

Get out there. Try meeting men whom you do not know. Be smart about it, of course. Never give out information that would compromise your anonymity until you feel perfectly safe doing so. Always expect to receive *his* information first. Do not continue with a man who will not come clean with you about his living situation and his marital status. He should give you *his* number first. If he is secretive about this, run the other way fast.

THINK SEXY

Remember to think in a sexy way. Don't put on an act. Just be your sexual self. Some of you may have sublimated this part of you. I have heard women say, "Oh, that part of my life is over." And then, five years later, I'm attending her wedding and hearing how she loves this man beyond anything either one ever imagined.

Life is wonderful that way. But not everyone has a happy ending. In fact, *no one* has a happy ending. We all die in the end. Not unless you fall asleep and drift off together into eternity will you avoid some heartache. Is it worth it to be happy for years at a time? Yes. A resounding "*yes*."

To me, sex makes a relationship whole. Of course there are couples that live in a sexless relationship by choice. That can suffice for some, perhaps even a large proportion of marriages. But many do enjoy sex. I find it hard to believe that we were given this joy producing ability and then not meant to use it for our whole lives.

Be grateful that your body needs a man. Do not hide this desire. You may find a partner where you least expect one. Be proud of your body and its working parts. Use it. Sex is good for your health. Stay active as long as you possibly can.

There are so many books on the subject of sex, some specifically for older women, such as *A Round Heeled Woman* by Jane Ruska, for one. Also, *Still Sexy After All These Years* by Leah Kliger and Deborah Nedelman, and *Still Doing It* by Joan Blank. There is a wonderful one called *She Comes First...* by Ian Kerner. It is a "how to" about giving a woman pleasure. Thank you, thank you, Ian Kerner. How wonderful that such a handbook has been written. Women should send him a thank you note.

Of course, not all of you will follow my advice about sex.

But some of you who may have been "on the fence" about this issue will hear these words and just give it a try. You will almost certainly surprise yourself.

Surely, at some time in your adult life, you were approached for sex by a husband or lover who was in the mood when you were not. Surely at least some of you at one time or another said, "Well, okay," knowing you would be giving pleasure to a man you loved but not expecting anything for yourself due to exhaustion or slight illness. Did it ever happen that you suddenly found you were turned on unexpectedly? Did you, in fact, enjoy yourself more than ever?

This can be translated into how your experiences with men work out now. You may suddenly become comfortable in the role of juicy older woman. I hope that you do. For I believe that the sex you enjoy in these years of wisdom and inspiration can surpass younger but less wise emotions by a mile.

If you are truly inhibited, there is help. Sex therapists can give you everything from pointers to drugs to enhance your love life. Find one and have a consultation. And don't wait until you have a guy. Start now on the road to happier and healthier sex. It may take a while to retrain your brain. And do expect a positive outcome.

Just as it is possible to change your mind about whether you are happy or sad, it is possible to change your mind about feeling sexy. It is all in your head. You can simply change your mind. It is that easy. Don't let a negative thought take hold.

WRITE IT DOWN

Write down what you feel you would like to do with a lover. Make it erotic. Don't hold back. What is your fantasy? Do you allow yourself to imagine a sexual romp with someone? Well, if you don't, then it is time to start. If you already know your desires, then write them down. Writing seems to imprint ideas more securely in the mind.

I say this over and over, yet sometimes women simply do not seem to hear it. *Write it down!*

Write down what you like about your body. If it pleases you, write down a list of pros and cons. But once you have admitted the bad things about your physical shape or your abilities to stretch or be flexible, then *let that go.*

You need not concentrate on the negative. Stay positive. Be grateful that you have eyes to see and the ability to write it down. Be grateful that you are able to think of your sexuality. Be especially grateful if you already feel sexy. Many women have stuffed their feelings so far down that they think they no longer experience them. Wrong. We are sexual beings. Only something like 1 percent of the population is really asexual. Everyone else is fully capable of responding to various stimuli.

Enjoy the game. Enjoy thinking sexy thoughts and giving your mind permission to roam on its own in this very fertile area. Frolic there. Of course, you know that I am going to suggest the Internet as a place where you can find anything you need in the way of sexual stimulus. You can find sites that describe and sell sex toys. You can find lingerie that will make you feel wonderful and brighten the eyes of a potential lover.

There are sites which show pictures of lovemaking. Many of these may be too graphic to actually stimulate a shy woman, or an inhibited one. Men use a more intense form of sexual voyeurism than women do. Many of the sites of which I speak are designed by and for men. Over and over again I will say, do not become discouraged if you do not find what you are looking for. Keep searching and you will discover things that *do* appeal to you.

Then, of course, there are sites where you can *meet* men for sex. I know that this sounds dangerous to women who have not tried it. But the safeguards in place make it relatively benign. I truly believe that this wonderful world of virtual sex helps create the mood you seek. This book is not a handbook for online sex, but there are such books. Try some.

You can go from a state of having *no* men in your life to having so many you can barely keep them straight. It is fun and educational to correspond with men who are also looking for the opposite sex.

And you can "get lucky," as the men say, and suddenly find yourself in the arms of a man who is really enjoying you as much as you are him.

The juices start to flow. You feel young and desirable. You are desirable. Just think how many single people there are out there. Slightly more than 50 percent of people in the USA are single. Help destroy this statistic. Find a mate on the Internet. You will be glad you did.

Chapter 5

Get Healthy

The most erroneous stories are those we think we know best—and therefore never scrutinize or question.
—Stephen Jay Gould, Paleontologist and Science Writer

Y ou are in control of your own health just as you are in control of almost everything about yourself. You may not believe this. Sometimes I have trouble believing it myself.

When you are trying to watch what you eat, don't you sometimes feel as if a little demon comes to you and makes you eat a piece of cake or a bowl of ice cream before you go to bed? It is as if we have a different personality living within us. So I certainly understand how you may feel when you begin to believe that you do not have control.

But, you do! It is a learned skill.

YOUR CHOICE

One of the most inspiring things that happened to me as I was writing this book was when Tiffany, my young assistant, said, almost dreamily, to me: "Aging is a learned behavior."

Yes! I said. *Yes*. That is exactly the point. We do not have to become old and decrepit as we age. We choose becoming that way, and often simply because we believe that is what is expected of us.

I have noticed that the women who truly never seem to age, often have no experience of their own mothers. Their mothers either died young or were absent for some other reason. Since these women never watched their own mothers age, they therefore did not have a pre-programmed idea of when they themselves should become old. Never having learned to be old, they simply skipped it.

Of course, genetics plays a part in whether you are healthy or not. Some people really seem to have sickly genes. But I believe that many others simply expect to be sick. And so they are. Health is in our heads. Just like sex. The healthiest part of our bodies must be our minds, or else we will surely become ill.

Medicine today is wonderful if you are broken in body. If you have an accident and need bones set, or skin sewn up, or burns treated, you should be thankful for all of our progress in medicine. For many other conditions, however, the healthcare system is not so helpful.

Today there is a whole file cabinet full of new diseases.

New conditions seem to be invented all the time. I just read somewhere that shopping to excess is now classified as a disease. That made me smile. The scientist who decided that was probably married to a shopper. Granted, there are compulsive behaviors that cause difficulties in a family. They may end a marriage.

They may make the person who deals with them very unhappy. But are they diseases?

Restless Leg Syndrome is an example of this. I do not doubt that there are some people who suffer from this. But which came first, the condition or the diagnosis? And if you watch television at all, you will be amazed at the number and variety of drugs advertised for sicknesses that were never heard of before this century. As I write this, the 21st century is only eight years old.

I choose health. I choose *not* to take all these drugs. If I die early, then so be it. I will not have clogged my body with drugs. I will at least know that it has really been me inhabiting my body. I will not have to take other drugs to counteract the drugs I have used to contain my diseases, according to the doctors.

You must question this culture of pill-taking to cure symptoms rather than lifestyle changes to eliminate disease. It is harder to change your life than pop a pill but, ultimately, it is much more effective in keeping you healthy. If you are the frugal sort, you may enjoy knowing that it is far cheaper to regain your health naturally than to take pills or other medication for the rest of your life. If you figure out what you have spent in the last ten years on sugary foods, alcohol, designer coffee, cigarettes (oh, yes...I know that some of you still smoke), or other toxic substances, you will be amazed. You could afford healthy gourmet meals every night instead. If you figure in the cost of medications as well, you will be staggered by the amount of money you are being asked to spend to stay symptom free (but not healthy) when the truth is, you can be healthy for the cost of whole foods.

Women of the 21st Century simply must begin to take responsibility for their own health. It is folly to expect the gov-

ernment to take care of you. That is *not* happening. If you have
ever been in the situation of having to depend on government-
mandated care, you will understand that it is not in your best
interest.

If you do not feel well, life becomes more difficult. Ideas
seem too difficult to put into effect. Tasks require too much effort. Life is empty and sad. So decide to take another look at
yourself and your health. How much of what ails you is your
own doing? Do you drink alcohol? Do you drink it too much?
Do you smoke? Do you eat fast food full of oils and trans-fatty
acids? Do you allow yourself enough sleep? Do you find yourself
constantly stressed? Do you live a life you enjoy? Do you harbor
resentments and anger? Do you take drugs for recreational enjoyment? And speaking of drugs, do you use prescription drugs
regularly?

In my view, everyone who takes drugs for an illness, whether
real or imagined, should seek a second and perhaps a third
opinion before doing so. And when asking advice about drugs,
do not expect to learn anything more from your doctor's partner than you do from him. You need an outside, uninvolved,
neutral party. Perhaps a different sort of health practitioner altogether. Drugs are pervasive in our society. I do not believe we
should be taking so many of them.

I am not a physician. Do not take my advice. But *do* question authority on this matter. Do seek new information. Stay
informed. Ask others who have taken what you are taking. Look
on the Internet for information. I read all the time about how
people must be careful of misinformation on the Internet. But
what about disinformation in your doctor's office? Not all doctors are forthcoming about side effects. Often drugs are used for
purposes that the drug company did *not* condone.

This has happened repeatedly in the childbirth world. *Cy-*

totec, a drug designed for ulcers, is used to thin the cervix in women ready to give birth to their babies. It can really help speed up the birth. That is true. But it can cause unendurable contractions at times, as well. Also, in about one in a hundred cases, it can cause uterine rupture. Yet doctors still use it. They do not tell their patients about the side effects. They do not tell them that the drug is not meant for this use at all.

Another example from the childbirth world involves not drugs, but surgery. Caesarian sections used to be rare. Or, at least, they used to be performed in under 10 percent of births. Now they are approaching 40, 50 even 60 per cent in many hospitals. This is outrageous. But one of the reasons it is happening is that it is easier to learn how to do a Caesarian than to learn all the tactics for assisting a baby that is stuck at the shoulders or having some other difficulty. It is simpler for the doctor to just cut the baby out. It is quicker, too.

Is a Caesarian Section better for the mother and the baby? No. But doctors are not going to worry about that when they could fit in more patients by doing one C-section after another. It is difficult to learn all those other techniques. It is time-consuming. And suppose they are not learned completely? In the past student doctors were taught methods for delivering problem babies. Shoulder *distocia*, breech births, various types of problems were mentioned and solutions sought. Not today. In fact, now they are simply taught the techniques of C-sections.

None of these new doctors have *ever* seen a home birth. Home is the only place where a true natural birth takes place. That is because at home the mother has everything she is familiar with. No one interferes with her wishes. No strangers touch her. There are no "rules" set by a hospital to satisfy an insurance company. The sense of peace is profound.

What a shame that this is no longer considered a safe place

to birth a baby. Because of this distorted perception, doctors see only an unnatural and medicated birth. Mothers are frightened. I believe that the doctors at these institutions are doing the best that they can, but they are going about it based on the information at hand. In Great Britain, it is recommended that women use a midwife unless the woman is high risk. The outcomes are better. A planned homebirth is as safe as hospital births. If this is the way your daughters want to birth their babies, be thankful, not afraid or disapproving. They are making a healthier choice and need your support.

Sex is Part of a Health

Libido—now there is a word to strike fear in the hearts of men over 50. The older they are, the more fear is attached to that word. I wonder if men realize that women are also afraid.

Many women feel that their ability to desire and be desired is over by 50. It is not. Sex is different in the second half of life—or call it the third half, if you wish. There is no doubt about it. The good news is, it is often better. If men judge good sex by how often or how long they are erect, then there is a decline in that sense. But women would *never* say that a man who is quick is a better lover than a man who is thorough (unless they hate sex).

What we hope, though, is that as men age, they learn by experience to do a better and better job of pleasing their partners, and, in doing so, they do a better job of pleasing themselves. Men gain a huge amount of pleasure from the reactions of the woman they are making love to. If the woman will react and give positive feedback, it causes the man to feel powerful and competent as a lover.

Men who come too fast never get to this. A man who is a bit

more worried about his own performance may put more effort into arousing his partner. He may be inclined to take more time about the entire performance. This is all a positive for women who take longer to arouse in any case.

Older women take even longer with the decades. Arousal is delayed in the late 80s and 90s. So far I have not spoken with a centenarian about this, but I hope I will soon. With older women, just stroking and kissing is often enough to make them feel loved. Sex is not just penetration. And with an older man, sometimes penetration with the penis is no longer possible. Dildos work fine. And so do fingers. A tongue may be best of all.

It is important for men to understand that the sex of their youth is not the best sex they ever had. They may find so much more satisfaction in their later years, because they are actually present while doing it. Young men sometimes just react, while older men need to make more of an effort throughout the act.

Dare to Be a Hundred is a wonderful book by Dr. Walter M. Bortz about growing older. Doctor Bortz discusses much of what I have said here. He is saying the same thing I am, which is "get a life, get out of the house, find something to do." He acknowledges that sex is part of health.

Do not think that it is a frivolous desire to enjoy sex. It is as necessary as food, water and sleep. Older people want and need sex. They may have issues surrounding it, but they need it just the same. Men have more difficulty in achieving an erection as they age. But if they feel sexy, there are many ways to show it besides penetration. For women, the issue is often finding partners. But in the 21st century, we have more options. Even though the number of men begins to dwindle as women reach their 80s and 90s, there are always men who are younger and turned on by being with older women.

TAKE CHARGE OF YOUR HEALTH

You are more likely to stay well if you are interested in life around you. Remain in the game. Do not retreat to the sidelines. Participate. Do not be a spectator in this. You *must* direct your own efforts in the direction you wish to go. The most important area for you to do this is in your own personal physical health. Do not depend on your yearly physical to do this. In fact, do not depend on anyone. You are the Master of your body. You are intelligent and, presumably, able to read. Do your own research.

I read somewhere that the most dangerous words in medicine are, "You are the doctor." Your doctor knows about disease, but he is looking for disease or sickness only as far as he knows. If he does not ask you questions about what is going on in your life and in your mind, he is missing the most important part of you for determining your diagnosis. Your body and its symptoms are just a clue to the doctor, not the final word.

In his book *Dare to Be a Hundred*, Dr. Bortz says, "Although death certificates cite heart attacks, stroke, or cancer as the cause of death, the real cause is usually smoking, excessive drinking, stress, bad diet or inactive lifestyle." In other words, the usual diagnoses are hiding the basic villains. Seventy percent of illness and death is attributable to behaviors that are yours to direct— and change.

"We become whole only by becoming old," says Dr. Bortz. "Only then do we develop swelling clarity." He says that, "dying young represents an incompletion." And he follows this with a wonderful quote by John Bradshaw: "Only in the evening can you know the whole day."

More people in their 90s are renewing their lives with new attitudes as well as new areas of interest. Life dries up when risk taking and new ideas cease to be a part of it. It is healthy to be afraid of the next step. If all you do is follow what you have always done, you will find at the end that you are nowhere. You must push yourself to explore new things, new places, and perhaps most important of all, new ideas.

One new idea is that you can direct much of what happens to your health. Sure, you may have a tendency for this, a predisposition for that, or a weakness somewhere, same as your grandmother had. But you already know about those tendencies and can often head them off with lifestyle changes. If your grandmother had bunions, spend some time early on wearing toe dividers, such as "yoga toes," to keep your toes healthily spread apart. If your grandfather had a heart attack at 50, try to discover why. If lifestyle was involved, change yours. Often supposedly bad luck illnesses and deaths are directly related to smoking, drinking, drugs and lifestyle in general. You choose. It will probably not happen to you if you decide to take control. Of course, some of these changes require great effort on your part. Do you want to live?

If you believe that your doctor knows more than you do about your own body, think again. You have the ability to monitor your body internally, thanks to your innate wisdom. I am not suggesting that you should never have a sonogram or have medical tests done. Not at all. But be careful. There are thousands of awful and sometimes fatal cases of medical mistakes. I *know* people personally who have been told that something showed up on a medical test that turned out not to be the case. Listen to your heart. Be skeptical. The nurses will support you. Doctors are not infallible. It is up to you to discover whether you feel comfortable with a treatment or not. You have the final say. Do your homework.

Recently, I heard about a distinguished physician who told a patient with Crohn's disease that she should not make any dietary changes. If she had a flare-up, the doctor simply told her: "Take the steroids." This was not some hack doctor of questionable degree. He is supposed to be one of the leaders in his field.

Be careful of a doctor who does not understand that food is medicine. Hopefully, this sort of healthcare professional is dying out. It is an established fact that diet has a direct effect on your health and can dramatically change the way you feel on any given day.

I repeat: It is important for you to have control of your life's direction. Those who feel a sense of control live happier and longer lives. As long as you can function—and a major test of late life is whether you can function—it does not matter a bit about a physician's diagnosis. You know what you can do.

And remember, it is not just having your health that makes your life worth living. Sadly, some healthy people live miserable lives, while unhealthy ones not only can be quite functional, they can be deliriously happy. Surely you know someone who is impaired in some way who still gets around quite well. You see blind people using guide dogs at events such as the symphony. Wheelchairs are common on our streets. These people are not "well" in the sense of being perfectly whole, but they are *very* well in that they are participating in life. They find joy in daily tasks, and they do most of the same things that you do every day.

Get out there and participate in life. That alone will keep you *ahead of the curve*.....

How to Stay Well

The basic steps to staying well are very simple, but the challenge comes when we go to carry out even the simplest of these basic directives. Here are my favorite 10—all lifestyle changes—that help keep me young:

1) *Have a strong spiritual belief system.* This does not include a religion that teaches hate or prejudice towards others. It definitely does not mean a religion that judges others. Using religion or spiritual beliefs to make yourself feel better than others is a sure way to sicken you and stunt your personal growth in life.

2) *Stay away from deep stressors, especially toxic relatives or friends.* However, keep some friendly stress in your life to keep you buoyed up and happy. It may be a sport that you love or simply games of chance, like Bridge or chess. Keep your mind stressed with pleasure, not with anxiety.

3) *Eat healthy food and drink lots of pure water.* No soft drinks, no sugar, no white flour in *anything*. Eat no processed foods, or at least severely limit them. By *severely*, I mean only eating them once or twice a month. For the very ill, I believe that the macrobiotic way, developed by Michio Kushi and available in books everywhere, is miraculously effective. On it, you must be vigilant. It only works if you follow it religiously.

4) *Get at least eight hours of sleep every night.* Do not allow yourself to become over-tired. Naps work. Take one today. And if you start to go to bed early, you will discover that it is a lovely experience. Waking up naturally without an alarm clock to the sounds of birds and morning sunlight filtering through your windows is one of the most unstressful things you can do for yourself.

5) *Exercise daily for at least an hour.* Walking is one of the simplest and most effective means of getting the body going. From there, you might want to take up more active modes of exercise. Dancing works for some people and others prefer an active sport like tennis, or fox hunting, or mountain climbing. The point is, do something.

6) *Stay emotionally close, whether to family or friends.* Do not

try to go through life friendless. At the very least, get a dog. It is most important to have someone you can physically touch, even if that someone is a dog or a cat. Something about skin on skin (or fur) works very well for the emotional and the physical release of tensions.

Seek out relationships with the opposite sex. If that suggestion stops you, read the chapter in this book on taking a lover before you go any further. It will help you to overcome your negative thinking that you are too old, too fat, too tired ... *Whatever*! There really *is* someone for everyone. Reach out with an open mind. As the years creep up, *everyone* has crow's feet and age spots. Forgive them and become friends. Do not fear meeting new people because you no longer look dewy and youthful. Be youthful on the inside where it really counts. You will attract others who are positive and young at heart. Being in the flow provides an exit for anxiety and boredom.

Remember, you are driving your life, you are not just a passenger. There are new adventures for body and mind in growing older. Steer toward them. Remember how much fun it was to acquire your first license to drive? Well, do that now. Drive your own life in the direction of health. The steering wheel is in your hands now! Don't give it to someone else. This is your life.

7) *Stay away from alcohol.* No Margaritas or Cosmopolitans allowed on this regimen! But I am a reasonable woman. No one needs to follow this plan every second, unless you are fighting a life-threatening disease. If you are, then no mistakes are allowed or recommended.

Wine in true moderation—as long as you are not an alcoholic—is probably a good thing, no more than perhaps four glasses a week. It probably does more good than harm. However, the disease of alcoholism is very prevalent, and if you have it, get help. Alcoholics Anonymous is the most effective organization by far for dealing with the problem. Go there and see for yourself. No one is turned away and the welcome you will receive may be the turning point in your life.

8) *Build Mental Muscle.* Never give up the quest for new knowledge. It will prove to be an advantage to you in every way.

Years ago, in the 1950s, it was believed that people could not build body muscle after a certain age. Generally, this limitation referred to the years after 40. Of course, this has proved to be ridiculous. But people used to believe it, just as they once believed the world was flat.

Now we know that not only can muscle be built up and added to—so can our brains. We have the capacity to build new mitochondria, the tiny powerhouse organelles inside our cells that convert molecules into energy when the cell needs it. Mitochondriae have their own little bit of DNA that tells them how to work and regulates them, which means is that our brains can gain new life if we will simply focus on learning new things at any age. Exercise is probably the most important ingredient when it comes to growing new brain cells. But so is diet and sleeping an adequate number of hours. We can build new brain cells, just as we can build new muscles, and that is a wonderful thing to know.

9) *Feel grateful every chance you get.* Gratitude is a life-affirming quality. We all need to take time *every day* to allow ourselves to feel grateful. We live in a special time, enjoying unbelievable "plenty." In general, we do not have to fear wild animals or difficult weather. We can go home to our snug houses and be warmed by central heating or cooled by air-conditioning. Most of us are not hungry or homeless. We are safe. We have at least a small circle of people who care about us. We have much for which to be grateful!

It always amazes me to think that most Americans live in a manner so luxurious as to be unimaginable to royalty, the kings and queens of centuries past. The fact that we can flick a switch and cause our rooms to be illuminated after dark would have been thought of as magic—if not impossible. The fact that we can drive a vehicle without hitching a horse, mule or oxen to a wagon would have been unheard of. The speed at which an automobile travels would not have been believed. Our ability to climb into a metal cylander and fly faster than sound to another destination, perhaps across an ocean, is a miracle compared to travel even 100 years ago.

The list goes on and on and includes the availability of a staggering array of foods in and out of season, many of which can be cooked in minutes or even seconds by microwave. The number of shoes in our closets, the pills, the phones, computers, artificial hips or knees, the information available—all this would have been completely beyond the reach of the most powerful emperor, who could never have begun to imagine what is available today.

Sometimes we forget how very much we have to be thankful for.

10) *Create your own rules.* "The earth is like a spaceship that didn't come with an operating manual," said Buckminster Fuller, underscoring how we have no set of directions for living life while on our journey here. We must create our own rules, our own set of instructions. The Bible, the Koran, and other wisdom literature handed down through the world's great religions offer us ways to deal with life's unknowns. But I am not speaking of religious direction here, nor do I think it is sacrilegious to apply some new rules to these later years. There are no precedents to follow—no operating manual—for life after

50, for the Baby Boomers and later generations who will live on into the 21st century.

As longevity continues to increase, people need guidance for how to live in this new reality. But I am not writing a manual for you so much as I am giving suggestions that you can follow. You have to be the judge of what is right for you and your lifestyle, and make your own rules. What I want you to remember is that you are in control. It is up to you. There is no operating manual, no instruction booklet to make it easier to navigate the unknown.

We have to find our own way, and many of us stumble into all sorts of troubles that we could have steered clear of if someone had taught us what to do. For instance, we are barraged with commercials on TV that extol the value of everything from vitamins made of poor ingredients, to medicines that would be totally unnecessary if our diets were correct to begin with. We are encouraged to stay up late to watch the news which comes on at a terrible time to be hit with blood and gore and hopelessness. We are taught to respect the opinions of learned men and women in positions of power. Have we forgotten what the '60s taught us?

QUESTION AUTHORITY

Why can't we do that when it comes to our health? Why can't we see that we must break the old mold and forge ahead in spite of what our grandmothers might have approved of for our age? This is a new millennium. The rules can change for the better. We are living longer. We are aging more slowly. I am not making this up. It is a fact.

We need to create our own rules. In fact there needn't be any rules, just suggestions. Each person may choose what they like and leave the rest, just as the slogan in Alcoholics Anonymous and Alanon says. Not everyone will want to jump out of a plane for their 80th birthday as George Bush did. But even someone who was less than healthy could be given a red chiffon scarf to wear, or buy herself a pair of brightly colored slacks. The point is color your life with adventures you did not have time to do in your earlier years. Color it literally or by deed.

Follow Common Sense

The directions for good health are available all around you. There are certain things that have been known for years about health and diet. It is easy to become educated, and much is just plain common sense.

But changing your diet and lifestyle is among the hardest things to do because so many of us are addicted to our bad habits, including eating sugar and refined wheat products. Cut them out. Yes. All of it. Never eat sugar or anything resembling "white powder" again. You surely know what this means. *None.* No salt except grey-ish sea salt. No white flour. No white sugar. I would like to add no "egg whites" of the powdered variety. If you want an egg, eat an egg. Nothing is healthier than eggs and avocados, two of the foods we are warned over and over again not to eat.

What about prescription drugs? You know what I'm going to say. Don't take them if you can help it. I am *not* a physician. But I have been watching for 65 years as fads come and go. When I was a child, the doctor who would come to our house for house calls in the late afternoon and give children a shot of antibiotic if we had a cold. My sister developed an allergy to sulfa from this too frequent practice. Too many shots, too young—and for nothing.

Times change, theories change. But good nutrition remains.

Eat good, whole foods. Do not buy prepackaged *anything*. Make your own prepared food, as much as possible. It is so much better and so much cheaper to do it that way.

Turn off the TV, and you will find that you have plenty of time.

Chapter 6

Get Up and Go

Only the educated are free.
—Epictetus, Greek philosopher

Exercise your rights and your body and your mind.
Get moving.

Get going.

Do not take no for an answer. Be proactive.

Whatever that means to you, do it.

Nothing is ever going to happen to you while you sit at home. Sitting at home worrying about how you will ever meet new people, or even that special someone, is pointless. Worrying is also pointless.

Get some perspective by getting out and going somewhere.

Get Out and About

Go somewhere by car or go on foot. Walking is the best, healthiest exercise there is. It makes you feel wonderful and look wonderful, too, and is right out your door. Nothing extra needs to be bought, no club membership or special clothes. Just go out there and look at the beauty of your environment. Enjoy your feet as they carry you all over the place.

Look where you are going. Don't just wear an iPod and forget that you are outside. The day is beautiful. Even if it is hot or cold. Simply dress appropriately. If it rains, wear a raincoat. You will feel so virtuous when you return home. No one will believe that you went out and walked in the rain. And you will establish that habit if you never skip a day.

Go *away*. Sometimes it is best to leave town and travel. Try something you have never done to get some perspective. Go somewhere you've never been, even if you hate to travel. Push the envelope.

There are so many ways to get away. Not all of them are expensive. Schools, museums and other organizations have all sorts of trips you may join. Some are surprisingly inexpensive, while others are a major investment. Pick a place you really want to visit. Try to find a trip that includes people you don't already know, but does include members of both sexes. Remember, it is often other women who introduce you to new men. It is less often other men who fix you up.

Explore exchanging houses with a friend or a stranger who may want to do the same. There are organizations that specialize in this. It is a good way to find what you are looking for and will cost you less money than you would spend on a hotel. You can find a place in another state or another country. Either one will be fine. Plan a weekend away. Borrow someone's house or apartment while they are away. Visit a city you have never been to. Read about travel. Plan a trip with a friend or go on a cruise if it is feasible. So many group trips are available.

Go.

Rise and Shine

I joined an exercise class that started at 6 AM three mornings a week. I began going to bed early so that I could wake up in time. The class really gave us a workout. Finishing at 7 AM made me feel wonderful, virtuous and energetic. I loved the class. I went to it for almost nine months. I would still be going, but my social life became so frenetic that I simply could not get to bed early enough. I welcome that kind of problem!

Can't get up that early? Here is a radical idea. Go to bed early and get a good night's rest. Really early. The hours that you sleep before midnight seem to have a double effect on your degree of restfulness during sleep.

Change your routine. Change your habits. *Do not watch television in the evening.* At all. It won't kill you. So many people stay up to watch the 11 o'clock news which obviously is going to make you go to bed late. Not only that, but the TV news may fill your pre-bedtime mind with images and thoughts that are disturbing and therefore not conducive to deep sleep.

You may think that I am advocating a PollyAnna type of "head-in-the-sand" attitude, but I am not. I am merely telling you to stop making it hard on yourself by surrounding yourself with negative vibrations. You can keep up with current events in the morning. Do not do it at night. In fact, you may discover that your life will be much more serene. Your sleep will be better. Your blood pressure will be lower. By the way, that early bedtime leads to wonderfully productive mornings. When you have extra time in the morning, your whole day goes well. You can accomplish more than you are accustomed to, and that increases your confidence and sense of accomplishment, fueling feelings of self-worth.

Another tip for a good night's sleep is this: do not eat dinner right before bed. It will keep you awake. Change your habit.

Remember we are speaking of change here. Perhaps you should skip dinner altogether and just have a light supper. A bowl of soup and a salad make a satisfying but not overly heavy evening meal. If you have a concern about your weight, this is definitely a way to improve things.

I believe that the number of hours that we sleep has a huge impact on our health and general well being. I make a point of sleeping eight hours whenever I can, and if, perchance, I need more sleep, I try to take naps or sleep in whenever it is possible. This has helped me stay healthy. If I do find myself feeling ill, sleep often makes the symptoms disappear, and I regain my health immediately.

Modern women (and men) often neglect this simple fact that sleep is vital for health. I once read that the necessity of using an alarm clock to wake up in the morning is a sign you are suffering from a lack of sleep. If you are sleeping enough, you won't need the alarm. This sounds amazing to many people, but I believe it. I no longer use an alarm clock except for emergencies, such as needing to wake at 4 AM to catch an early plane.

GET OUT OF YOUR COMFORT ZONE

Boredom can be a problem. It sometimes masks itself so well that you don't even know you are bored. You yawn or fidget or simply "space out." Repetitive and familiar tasks can become boring, even as they seem "normal" or easy.

Sometimes you need to shake yourself up. Change your routine. Create a new reality. Does this sound like too much work?

Have you the desire to change? That may be the first step. Change takes effort. So you need to be very clear about whether you really want to go that extra mile. However, if you don't, then you must stop complaining about how your life is unsatisfying and you never have anything wonderful happening in your life.

Oh, how I wish I could make you understand how *very* much of the life you experience is in your own hands! We *do* control what happens to us. Our thoughts direct the lives we are living. We have such power that I believe we actually do need to be careful what we wish for—and ready to have it.

So many people have yet to embrace this belief. But it is the most empowering attitude you can have in life. If you think that everything "happens to you," then you will be an eternal victim of life, and neither I nor anyone else will be able to help you change your life. If you are not willing to open your mind to the possibility that you can make the changes you need—just open to the *possibility*—then save your eyesight. Stop reading this book and go outside for a walk. It will do you more good.

CLEAR YOUR MIND

If you believe you can be the architect of your own future, then anything you can do that will clear your mind will be beneficial. With a clear mind you may discover that the ideas start floating by. Catch a few of them and keep your favorites. I often have to speak into a recorder or stop and jot down inspiring ideas that come to me, or else I forget the substance of these "gifts" from the Universe. Sometimes I marvel at their simplicity and at how obvious these thoughts are as they occur. And I often marvel that I failed to think of these things while sitting at my desk, "working" on some creative project.

Some people prefer the cleansing effect of water to clear their minds for creative and inspirational thinking. I know several people who get their most profound ideas while in the shower. Their showers are long and mentally cleansing. Some people soak in the tub. Whatever frees your mind, do it. Swimming is doubly helpful, both meditative and a wonderful exercise.

It is in freeing yourself from mundane patterns of life that, suddenly and easily, new ideas come up and have a clear spot to land. Enjoy them. Cultivate and care for them. These are the guiding forces that can shape and change your life for the better. Collect as many as you can.

Maybe all this talk of change is making you feel tired. Often when the subject is awkward or "hits a nerve" in our psyches, we react by feeling tired. It makes us uncomfortable, and besides, the idea of change frankly terrifies us. It literally destroys our ability to move forward. We must push past that feeling of ennui and fear. We must simply say, *NO, I will not repeat patterns that lead to unhappiness and blockage in my progress.*

A PASSION FOR CHANGE

I think change of any kind is one of the hardest things to implement. You tend to eat the same things because you always buy the same things when you shop at the market. You buy these things because you like them. Some of them may be simply terrible for you, but you have eaten them since childhood. They make you feel good. They offer security and familiarity.

Try something new. Buy something you have never bought before. Try an Asian vegetable or a cut of meat with which you are unfamiliar. Buy rabbit or grouse or try a grain with a name that is new to you—*spelt* or *kamut,* or *quinoa.* Read the instructions for cooking, because some of these foods do not require the same amount of time to cook as items you are familiar with.

All of this simply prepares you to change. One tiny change shows you the way. Confidence comes with one change, then one more brings more. "If I can do this, I can do another. And later, "If I can do this, I can do anything!"

Build new habits slowly, but never stop. Sudden multiple changes usually do not last. One at a time seems most successful. Don't hesitate to try more than one if you feel you can. Some changes go together, like turning off the TV and going for a walk. Or eating earlier and going to bed at an unusually early hour.

So now we are going to charge on to consider even larger ideas of change.

Change Your Address

Have you considered moving to a new town? Oh, yes you could. People have a tendency to stay put even though they are unhappy or unfulfilled. Why? I can just hear the arguments. "My job is here, my house is not paid for, my children are in school here." Considerations must be made for practical reasons. "I cannot afford to move." However, fear often causes blindness to other options. Sometimes I tell people, "You cannot afford *not* to move."

Don't worry. I am not suggesting that each one of you reading this pull up stakes and move across the country. It simply bears thinking about. Would a move help you? Would it spur you on to greater happiness? What causes you to feel happiness? Do you know the answer to this?

It seems difficult to imagine how many people do *not* know what makes them happy. They know they want their credit card debt paid off. But they do not seem to know what would make them happy. They would like their boss to acknowledge them, but what would be the point of this if the job did not make them happy?

This is one of the times when I recommend a book such as *The Secret* (http://www.thesecret.tv/)for a quick fix, or *A Course in Miracles (http://www.acim.org/)*, if you're willing to really study. These books will change your life. This is heady stuff. Are you ready? Some people welcome new ideas, while others call them "occult," New Age, or just enlightened. However you view these ideas, do not repudiate them without giving them a fair trial. Read *everything* you can find about the Law of Attraction. It works. Dr. Joe Vitale's program called *The Missing Secret (http://www.missingsecret.info/)* is one of the most clearly stated, helpful and thoughtful programs of its kind. You can check it out at www.missingsecret.info. If you will buy, borrow or...well, don't steal it, but do practice it!—it will transform your life in the most positive way. Vitale has a very clear style that makes it easy to follow his directions and empathize with his stories and examples.

GET EDUCATED

It is *never* too late. You will enjoy it. It will make you desirable. Don't just change your body. Let your mind join in. Take stock of where your education left off. Schools now have classes for everyone. Many universities are more than half "non-traditional" students. You never have to feel out of place going back to school. You can major in a course of study completely new, different, and interesting to you now. You can fulfill that youthful fantasy that you abandoned because you needed to be practical and make money. Now, perhaps, money is not the highest priority.

What makes your brain smile when you think of learning more? What did you want to do when you were a child? What did you want to be when you "grew up"? Did you dream of being a doctor? Or were you more interested in being a policewoman or a mother, or a nurse...? What was it that made that attractive to you? Did you like the uniform? Or was there an underlying theme and emotion?

Anthony Robbins, the famous motivational speaker and author, uses this inquiry in his talks about finding a purpose for one's life. He suggests that you write down what you wanted to be as a child and what it was that you expected to get from that job or career. It might be helping others or healing others—or even robbing others! But whatever it is, you can still get the essential feeling you were looking for back then by simply finding a different profession that allows you to experience that sort of feeling.

Discover all the different ways to get an education now, from an online course on the Internet to enrolling in a class at a local school, or job-related classes. Everything you need to know about finding a way to educate yourself is on *Google*. It is a lot easier than it once was. Read about it. Never think it is too late or that it will take too long. Time passes whether you are in school or not. It is amazing how quickly time passes. Start *now*. Look into "distance learning" for chances to study and get degrees at universities that have such programs. Check out local community colleges. That is a great way to start. These non-threatening schools are designed to allow people to ease into the learning mode. They are varied and many. Universities have programs where seniors over a certain age—60 or so, but sometimes even younger—can study for free or for a much-reduced tuition. Start there.

Once I could not type. So someone suggested a computer program called *Mavis Beacham Teaches Typing*. I bought it and installed it. The directions asked me what my age range was. The youngest age was 4-8 years old. I said that was my range. I wanted to be sure I learned from scratch. It took me several months of taking lessons every night, but I became a passable typist, typing about 48 words a minute. This seemed a miracle to me.

But learning to type is simply muscle memory. You can do it, too. Believe me, if I could do it, so can you. What do you wish that you had studied? Is there something new to study that was not available when you went to school the first time, such as IT training or cutting-edge psychology techniques?

I went back to college at age 50. I had to start from scratch since I married so young and began having babies right away. It was frightening. I was terrified. So I took one course at a local community college. I was so scared during the course that I had no idea whether I was doing well or not. When I received an "A" for the course, I was shocked and pleased. I did it. And if I could do it once, I can do it again. Soon I enrolled in a large state university. It was the best decision I could have made. It gave me confidence. It opened my eyes to the world we live in today. And I took more courses than I needed to in order to graduate.

EXPLORE A NEW CAREER

Start with something brand new. There are so many new technologies. There are refinements on old technologies. Film, for instance, once the province of Hollywood or big studios around the world, now brings together all sorts of independent artists. Leveling the playing field has brought the players in contact with each other.

Do you have a passion for something? That can give you a "leg up" on any job. I always suggest volunteering to work at something you really care about. Volunteering for an organization serves two purposes. One, it allows you to discover whether you are really interested in the day-to-day workings of this type of organization; and two, it gives you an insider's view of upcoming positions at the company or organization where you volunteer.

Decide what you want your life to be and make it happen.

You have so much more control over this than you may think. What you think is vital. You really can change yourself. No one else can. Your thoughts determine who you are and what you will become. Practice good thinking.

Imagine who you would like to become. If you are not sure, get some ideas by reading and talking to people. Watch appropriate TV shows or movies, or go to live entertainment. Or a club. Volunteer. Do something for someone else. This opens doors to feelings and events you may have no idea could be in your future. These events cannot be predicted.

The universe allows us to expand our limits beyond anything we can imagine if we just allow it. The benefits of taking yourself out of comfortable surroundings and venturing out into the world cannot be overstated. Join a book club. Join a group or an organization that demands some sort of mental activity. Go to an opening or a fund raiser. Seek out people who are involved in dynamic activities. Their energy will increase your own. Stay with those whose energy is positive.

Do not let others dictate your fate with their negativity or doom and gloom. I am aware that it is possible to become depressed. I have felt it. I have fought it. Sometimes it is necessary to push yourself to climb up out of the doldrums. But you can do it. Smile. Watch a DVD that makes you laugh. You will be amazed at how it can change the way you feel if you just start to think in a positive way. It is not cheating to take a shortcut to be happy.

CHOOSE POSITIVE PEOPLE

Do you have a friend or relative who keeps you feeling disappointed or blue? Begin to shed yourself of negative influences from friends. Sometimes it is a good idea to see less of some family members. Wait until you are stronger. Stay with people who make you laugh. Surround yourself with people who make you feel powerful and competent.

Be ruthless about this. I cannot emphasize enough the power that others have over your moods. Of course, you must keep in touch with your family. You can acknowledge them, but then avoid any unnecessary contact if they are distracting you from your mission to stay positive. Be vigilant. Be firm in your denial of all negative influences over you.

Never listen to CountryWestern songs when freshly heart-broken. They are so adept at picking up on anguish that you may become addicted to them. They just reinforce your pain. Wait till you have the inner strength to listen to them. Even if you have a favorite, try to defang it by playing it only at certain times. Allow yourself a few minutes sometime in your day to listen to a song that breaks your heart anew, but do not let it infuse your thoughts all day long. Stay away from things that remind you of what is hurting you.

It is very important not to make yourself unhappy. You may feel that your life is hard and that others have mistreated you. But get over this as fast as you can. You must go forward without holding on to resentments and old hurts. Not only is holding on a waste of time, but in thinking of the negative, you constantly reinforce it. Keep it out of your thoughts.

LET GO OF NEGATIVITY

We can reinforce positive thoughts by the same method that we allowed our negative thoughts to dominate our thinking. In this case, you must think of the positive thing repeatedly. You will be amazed at how turning these positive thoughts over and over in your mind allows them to strengthen and grow pervasive. Once the good thoughts have gained power, you will discover that the foul ones have lost their power to bother you.

You can always replace one set of thoughts with another, one type of action with another one. In fact that is the key to breaking a habit. You must replace the old with a new action. This goes for thoughts as well. We are in control of our thoughts, not the other way around.

Sometimes we forget this reality. I have chewed day and night on painful memories. I myself am not by any means immune to this. However, wisdom has shown me that I am the one who decides what I will think about. It really is possible to force the mind away from hurt and focus on enjoyment.

It helps, in the beginning, to use props. I suggest funny movies or even funny books. Books take more effort to read than movies do to watch. So if you are paralyzed with devastating pain from some emotional drubbing, you might just put in a comedy DVD. You can just lie on our couch or bed and watch it. No effort is necessary. Eventually something will strike you as funny. You will find yourself laughing in spite of raw nerves and even in spite of tears. Keep watching. Each time you laugh, it has a physiological impact on your brain. You are actually changing your brain chemistry when you laugh. Even a smile works this way. So try to do both often.

Books on tape or CD work well for this. You can listen to them in your car as you commute to work. You do not have to think of anything but the words being spoken to you through your car's sound system. Do this often. Ask friends for suggestions of funny novels or biographies. Do not listen to dark comedy that relies on negative gags. Stay away from ethnic humor unless you really know you like it. Teasing others in a negative way can be destructive. You will find that it suddenly feels good to laugh. You will get a sort of "high" from feeling good. Use this to help heal a broken heart. You can make a broken heart last for years or you can make it heal much more quickly.

BE YOURSELF

When you ratchet up your own comfort zone to expand and become who you truly are, you can feel comfortable in your own skin.

When I was first separated, it was a difficult time for me. I hated giving up my status as a married—and *happily*, at that—woman. But it was a time when I felt explanations were in order because of the total confusion exhibited by our friends and acquaintances. I certainly did it with my head held high, but it took an effort that I no longer need to exert. At that time, I was thinking that I had to act a certain way to make the transition. I really worked it. Partly it was a pride thing. But it was also to try to relieve that curiosity and shock that people sometimes feel about a couple that splits up with no apparent reason.

To help make the transition and not be marginalized by the world at large, I gave parties every month as I mentioned before. I did that for over two years. It was a goal I set for myself, my way of being proactive. I enjoyed thinking up reasons to have these parties. Some were very simple; a few were truly complicated and expensive.

Finally, I have given myself leave to stop giving parties. Now, instead I am going out a lot, feeling very comfortable, and I am receiving a lot of invitations from people whom I entertained in the past two years or so.

What I'm doing is not so unusual. And neither is what I'm urging you to do. You're not starting from scratch. You have wisdom and experience, so not really "from nothing" are you building your new life. Think of the process as similar to what you do with a set of building blocks. You may build an elaborate castle for a child who knocks it down immediately. But the building blocks are still there, even though they are disassembled. And you can build them back up again. If that does not suit you, you can knock them down and build again. You can start again, and again, and again. In our world of long-lived men and women, we must expect that rebuilding and reinventing our lives will be the norm rather than the exception.

ALL ABOUT ATTITUDE

One thing that influences how you feel about your own aging is your personal view of how others age. If all you see are sick old people, you may feel that sickness is going to be your lot. I recommend finding some healthy people much older than you are to observe. There are plenty of them. I hope that in our lifetime there will be many more.

One man whom I have known for years is still hunting hounds at the age of 84. He inspires me. It is no easy feat to prepare and dress for hunting, mount your horse and ride over land that you may not have seen before while listening for hounds and judging where the fox may be. This man remains one-of-a-kind. But for all those who are younger than he, he is a beacon. His example will lead many others to refrain from hanging up their spurs and quitting, perhaps in their 70s.

All sports have inspirational people like this. Whatever you like to do, find someone much older than you to be your mentor and example. Half of living long and healthily is knowing that you can.

Today I visited an older couple who live in their own home with nurses round the clock. They are fortunate that they can afford such a life. They are also a great example of how a couple can live together for more than 70 years and still want to hold hands as they welcome their children and grandchildren around them.

Many women feel that at a certain age they can no longer do what they used to love doing. Sports especially seem out of reach if one stops too soon. The idea of getting back in seems insurmountable. But it is not.

Cultivate new friends to enjoy a sport if your old ones have decided to stop. Do not stop doing what you love. Recently, a man I knew died at the age of 92. He had a heart attack while playing in his weekly doubles tennis game. Not a bad way to go!

Years ago my grandfather-in-law loved to sail by himself. His children were scandalized by this. They wanted to put a stop to it. But he loved it. He did manage to sail, into his late 80s. He never did injure himself. He died of an illness at the age of 87. I always felt that it was more important for him to sail, even if there was a risk that he could die. If he had lost his life doing what he loved, he would have counted himself lucky. As it was, he eventually died in bed.

TRIBES

Now, some of my philosophical but practical advice about how to become unstoppable, because you already are. I believe that we are constantly traveling in our familiar packs and tribes throughout life after life. Throughout eons, throughout history, we keep coming back until we have evolved to the point where we no longer have any issues left to work out.

Reincarnation feels right to me. I do not expect that everyone must believe what I believe. Each person must find a spiritual place that feels right to him or her. But if you will indulge me for a minute, I will tell you what I believe to be true.

We travel with the same people as we reincarnate. We have a tribe, and we navigate this life together to heal, to learn, to complete relationships together. In so many ways, we are all related. It helps my life to make sense when I believe this. I find it immensely comforting and it helps explain a lot of the unexplainable.

Do we really die? And then there's nothing? To me, that belief is truly sad. If people could just relax and let go of guilt and fear, I believe they could accept that it's obvious it doesn't all just end.

Of course, Christians don't believe it just ends, because they believe in Heaven and Hell. But I believe we are all evolving now at this level of earthly existence, and many are ahead of me. I've always resisted going to the next level, because I like my earthy nature, and I fear becoming too highly evolved to enjoy all my earthly pleasures.

One day I will be ready, but not yet.

CHAPTER 7

PARE DOWN

If our minds and hearts are too full of memories of the past, there is no room left for the pleasures of tomorrow.
—BONNIE B. MATHESON, COACH AND AUTHOR

There is an ancient secret that Western women (and men) need to learn: We are weighted down by our own *stuff*, a condition that robs us of vitality, energy, ease and joy in life.

TOSS JUNK, GAIN ENERGY

Here is a little-known energy producer that is easy and free. Start with one dresser drawer and throw away things you do not use. Give away things you no longer want. Sell things that someone else might find a treasure. The Chinese have the right idea about things. One or two treasures beautifully displayed make much more impact than a houseful. Too many things get in your way. Do not allow this. You will discover that a huge weight is lifted from your shoulders if you pare down and own fewer things. You will have more energy.

Junk takes up space in your closets and in your mind. Throw it out. If you can begin to clean up shelves in your bathroom or closets, you will see almost immediately how it frees you mentally as well as physically. It becomes easier and easier to discard things once you start. Get some boxes or suitcases and begin putting things into them. The ultimate goal is to throw out everything that you are not using. In the beginning, you can simply set no longer-needed items aside.

Discard any clothes that do not fit or are out of style. This is so easy. Why do I have so much trouble with it? I start to toss, and then I think, *Oh, I might wear that if I had a costume party to go to.* Wrong. Toss it out. When you find yourself with extra hangers because you have thrown out so many things that your closet is beginning to look like someone else's, you know you are on the right track. Are there things in there that have been unworn for a decade? *Move them out.* You can save them in a box somewhere for a few months—if you must. But think about whether you really miss them. If you do, then you can get them back.

Do not fear tossing things out. If you simply remove them from your sight, or site—it will work wonders. Do not confuse any lack of enthusiasm for tossing with character flaws.

You have a purpose in life. You have goals to fulfill. You are perfect as you are. Love yourself enough to enjoy yourself. Love yourself enough to save your sanity and your energy for the work you are meant to do.

As you carve yourself out of all the stuff in your life, you will uncover the part of yourself that has been neglected. You will find your dream, hidden perhaps among all that *stuff,* some of it being the obligations to friends and family that do not serve you.

Extricate that dream. Nourish it. The more you concentrate

on your goals, the more you will realize exactly what they are. This is the time for you to find out what really needs your attention. This is the time to follow your dreams. Neglected dreams do not die. They get shelved and, sometimes, forgotten. Do something about them now.

Pare down!

This second half of your life lends itself to new discoveries and new frontiers, so clear the way. Don't ever hear yourself say, "It is too late." Do not think it. Even if you are not able to realize the dreams of youth exactly, you may be able to do something that makes your heart sing. If you always wished to be a doctor, look into joining your local rescue squad. They have programs to teach you to do the kinds of things you wanted to do in your dream of becoming a doctor.

Clear away old junk and with it your ideas of "lack," and find new ways to experience that part of you that has been dormant. Are you artistic? Did someone tell you that you had no talent? Once I believed I could not write because of a remark a teacher made to me when I was 18. For years, I believed he was right, and I was wrong. It was not until I was 50 that a different teacher led me to see that I can write in a clear and concise manner. From her encouragement, I have evolved into a writer and a motivational speaker.

Clearing out that old message of "I can't" took me years. Yet I have been happier at my computer, simply putting words on paper, than almost anywhere else. In order to find time to write, I have rearranged my life to make a place for it. This seemed impossible at first. I sold a business and set out on my own to try to find the words to help other women like me. I have a strong desire to aid women in their journey through life.

My premise that women will live to be 100 or more involves *you.* Listen to me. I am living what I write about. My life is completely changed from my earlier expectations, and I am more content than I ever expected to be. This happened because I took the time to carve out the space, make room for a different kind of life. It's really an ongoing process. The adventure has only begun.

Cleaning Out Your House, Your Life

When trying to clean out your house or apartment, you must be focused. It is difficult. Sometimes it hurts to find old mementos of a life that is past, gone forever.

But if that is true for you, set mementos and other hard-to-throw-away items aside in a place where you may be brave enough to just get rid of them later. Some items seem to have a life of their own. You are in control of your feelings. Stay steady. Do not let emotions keep you from clearing clutter from your life.

Many women who are in their last decade of a century find it almost impossible to throw anything away. They are paralyzed by the things that seem to be most alive with memories. They cling to them in an almost unnatural way. Because of this, I suggest you try to pare away your excess possessions before that time in your life when you no longer can.

There is real power in having empty space in your life. Giving yourself empty space in which to live allows a positive energy to enter your life. It is like taking a vacation, both liberating and relaxing. What is difficult is beginning to do it. Just like any task it begins with a single gesture, a single step. Finding the energy to take that step is the hardest part. Fear of change keeps us trapped in our belongings for years, maybe forever. Strip away the fear and find the organized person hiding under there.

When you start on a new room or even a new drawer, remember to plan a reward for yourself. Whether it is dinner out at a favorite restaurant or an hour lying on the couch with a magazine, be kind to yourself. It takes guts and energy to clean out old parts of your life. Sometimes the only way to motivate yourself is with a reward.

Sometimes just deciding to do it makes you tired and the work must be put off for a better time. For some of us our energy really does lessen as we age. At least it sometimes seems this way. Even though we may hate to admit it, we do learn to hoard our strength. We are used to making small concessions to our dwindling store of adrenalin. We do not carry the heavy boxes—we drag them. Or we purposely put things in smaller boxes so that we can move them once they are packed. Using our wisdom to make the physical tasks lighter can increase our mental energy by quite a lot.

The post-menopausal zest that anthropologist Margaret Mead spoke of is real. So do not expect to have less energy as you pass that point, so much as a different type. You will be able to do exactly what you believe you can do. As always, it is up to you. The power is in your hands.

If you have children or grandchildren, consider giving away memories—mementos—to them. It is better for them to be given something while you are both still alive. That way you can tell the recipient what it is that you are giving them. It may be much more complicated later, if and when the gift appears by itself, unexplained by the giver. I believe our possessions have some aspect of us attached to them. When you give them away you are giving a tiny part of yourself. It is really a gift to be cherished. Enjoy watching the gift work its magic while you still can.

You may wish to move to a new address. Many people keep up a lifestyle that is no longer working for them, simply because they are used to it. Sometimes it is because you are afraid of the nuisance of having to pack up and move.

On the other hand, some people move too soon. Be careful to understand what it is that you need in a habitat. Do you need lots of space? Do you need quiet? Do you need people around you? Do you enjoy organized activity? Do you still drive? Do you wish to walk to all your shopping needs?

What about pets? Do you have a dog? Or perhaps you own several dogs or several cats, or something more exotic? Think about what it means to move these. Will they be safe? Will they be happy? What else should you do to prepare pets for a move?

Many people move to areas where they will be closer to their children, but no matter what is your motivation, it is extremely upsetting to move. While I am suggesting that you think about a move, I am very aware of the trauma attached to moving. It is wrenching. Think twice about whether you are ready to do this.

In fact, it may be so liberating to simply clear out the clutter in your house, you won't need to move to simplify your life. You do not need to find a new nest if you can make your old one fresh and pleasant for your current lifestyle.

Some women find that keeping a house they have lived in for years can be simplified by renting out some space in the house to someone else. This can give some security and safety as well as company. Or it can be a huge nuisance. Do not do anything in haste. It is important to remember to never move or make decisions about your space within the first year of the death of a spouse. Wait. Give yourself time to grieve in familiar territory.

You may have some ideas deep inside your mind about where you would like to live. Try to be quiet and listen to your inner voices, and learn what it is that you really want. Be vigilant. Do not take others' word for it.

Write It Down. As in creating anything new, the first step is to write what you want in a notebook. At the same time, visualize it often. Think of tiny details. You may be amazed at how nearly you are able to realize this dream if you will make it solid by thinking about it in detail and writing it down—or pasting pictures of what you like—in a book.

Making a Vision Board solidifies your desires in a visual way that can be fun as well as effective. Buy an inexpensive poster board large enough to put many photos, pictures from catalogues, drawings, or written descriptions of what you wish for. Anything will do. You can decorate it, embellish it and have fun doing it. Keep it within your daily viewing space. Look at it often.

We can visualize what we want and make it happen. The best that we can do is all we can expect of ourselves. But that best is so much better than many people realize. We have huge power to create our own reality. I can't emphasize this too often, and neither should you. Do not settle for what someone else says you must.

Of course, you must take action. Make it happen. Set the stage and then set events in motion.

PARING DOWN PEOPLE

Now here's a challenge that yields huge additional reserves of energy, if you can do it. Discard those people in your life who are not conducive to your happiness. This may sound brutal. It may also be or seem impossible. But think about doing it anyway. How many so-called friends do you have who are leaches and spongers? How many family members bother you so much that you avoid holidays with them? Which of your children or in-laws hurts you repeatedly with their words or their lack of caring for you?

Think about what you can do to trim your life of stress-producing people. You may be surprised to find that you can clear some of them away by just failing to connect with them when it is their expectation that you do. You are not under a contract to answer the phone every time it rings! Get caller ID and let it work for you. Do not feel guilty about saving yourself or your energy. Later, when it suits your schedule and if it suits your relationship, sit down and have a good talk with people about why you can't spend more time (or any) with them. Be responsible and don't blame them. You are in charge of your life!

Sometimes paring down people in our lives can be more difficult than throwing out things. How can we relegate people whom we know to the dust bin? Well, the truth is, it may be necessary to save our lives. Your sanity and your peace of mind is important. You have a right to both. Over the years, we can become weighed down by people whom we have no idea how to leave.

It is important to learn the skill of letting go. It is so important to clean house internally as well as really cleaning our closets. Much of what we clutter our minds with is simply flotsam and jetsam that we do not need. We need to get rid of it all. Why do we cling to ideas and old memories as if our lives depend on them?

LETTING GO

We can start fresh. We can simply make a decision to move on. Of course, moving on means we are no longer able to blame our failures on old hurts and resentments.

Ah, resentments! More than anything else they are the stumbling blocks to our personal growth. The very word *resentment* is poison. Pluck out resentments as if they were thorns under the saddle of our most valued steeds. We cannot make progress when we are galled by these cantankerous memories. We must agree within ourselves to leave the past *in the past,* where it belongs.

So often our old resentments are a familiar source of inner turmoil. They are familiar and almost friendly. We are so used to them that when they are gone, we feel their lack. We also feel lighter and freer and ready to go further, faster. When we replace something disagreeable, it helps. Replace your negative influences with positive ones. Do this without fail. It almost never works to simply give something up, leaving a void. Much more effective is the method of replacing one vice with another habit that is positive. This is even more important with people. Try to surround yourself with those whose outlook is sunny.

It may be comforting to know that whatever has happened to us, others have had worse to deal with. We must go forward with clean souls. We must not waste one ounce of energy on old sores. Just as we would clear our shoes of pebbles, or our face of accumulated dirt, we must scrape off the residue of past slights and step forward unencumbered by extraneous irritants.

Paring down can include letting go of old family hurts. So many of us are still harboring resentments against our parents or others who harmed us as children. Often these incidents were inadvertent, not intentional. The perpetrators knew nothing of what they did.

Times have changed.

When I watch young parents today explaining away every hurt their child may encounter, I wonder at the change in attitude from when I was young. Then children were expected to obey above all else. Our feelings were often not considered worthy of note. If we felt bad, whatever caused it was probably for our own good. Or so they told us.

It was even more so for the generation before ours. As a

child, my mother had to leave her dog every fall when her family would move back to Washington, D.C. for the school year. She longed for her dog all through the year and only saw him at Christmas and during the summer months. She suffered terribly. As an only child, her dog was an important part of her family. She missed the dog as she might have missed her mother had she been alive. Once she was an adult, my mother was so scarred by this experience that she insisted on taking her dog with her everywhere.

Yesterday, I spoke to a woman in her 80s who remarked about how hard it was for children to know what their talents were in those days. Many affluent families had nannies who saw to the education of the children. The child might be artistic, but if recognizing that was not part of a nanny's education, then the child in her care might not ever be able to discover his or her own talent.

Many children were considered stupid if they had trouble learning how to read. Now we understand childhood disabilities such as Attention Deficit Disorder, dyslexia, even being left-handed! In the 20th century, many a left-handed child was forced to learn to write with the right hand. Sometimes the left hand was tied down to avoid any possibility of using it. Seventy-five years ago, those same children who are aided by doctors and therapists today were relegated to the dunce's corner. It frightens me to think of the damage done by well-meaning experts. And it humbles me to know that, even now, much of what we think we are doing right when it comes to raising children may one day be written up in case studies as complete balderdash.

Keep an open mind, but trust your instincts more than anything else.

MAKE THAT SPACE!

Back to my point: You must make a space for the things you wish for in the future if you truly want them to happen. In order to write a book, for instance, one must find a way to write every day, even if there is nothing to say at that moment. Of course, the reality is that I have procrastinated over and over, thereby wasting a lot of time. Still, I have forced myself to write it down, bit by bit.

It is the same with paring down the things in your house and people in your life. You must simply do it. Don't wait until you are ready to do it. Do it *now*.

You will have some good days and some bad days. Keep thinking of the space you will create for new things in your life. If you do not do this, you will constantly block the Universe from giving you what you want.

If you live to be 100, you had better find a way to make way for all those many years' worth of new things. Were you ever taught that you might have 100 years to live? I certainly was not. Years ago, my young husband told me he expected to live to be 100. That was the first time I had ever thought of such a thing. It seemed a crazy idea at the time. We were 20 years old, and even 50 sounded old to me.

Now that I am well over 60, I am not so horrified by the idea of living for a century. The important thing is to make sure that you can be healthy. That is more possible now than ever. Our joints can be replaced, our hair dyed and enhanced with extensions and added tresses. Our eyes can be improved, our faces lifted, our bones strengthened. We will not be the same women our grandmothers were in our 70s, 80s or 90s.

Once over 100, there is not so much known. I believe that in years to come, the first 10 years after 100 will equate with what we once thought of as 80. Who knows how long we may live. Like the four-minute mile, the common belief that we are not able to live much past 100 may simply be just that, a belief.

We are told that our physical bodies simply cannot go on. Our systems will break down. Our genetic makeup programs us to die. What if that is as wrong as was the statement that we could not grow more muscles after a certain age? What if it turns out to be as wrong as the theory that we could not grow more brains cells after a certain age? Over and over you will hear me say, "Keep an open mind." For you just do not know.

What if we have pared down our relationships to zero? If we are single, we may open ourselves to a new relationship because we are available. Single, we are a target for any man who is looking for a partner. Many of you will choose to stay alone. Either way, it is your choice. Just remember that phrase, *When the Lord closes a door, He opens a window*. Whether you are religious or not, the essence of these words is true. When we create space, the Universe will help us fill it. It is up to you to be selective in that filling.

Remember, you are in control of your own choices. You are in control of what you fill your life with. Choose carefully. Life is long. Do not assume anything you ever heard about aging is true.

All the rules are changed.

STAY AWARE OF YOUR WORLD

So many things we once thought of as normal are gone forever, and shocking things are the norm. Social behavior and patterns are altered by the dramatic increase in population, as the baby boomer generation matures. For example, our huge jump in population has made it necessary to use caution about planning events or meetings at "rush hour" to avoid wasting time stuck in traffic. Even worse, the great surge in numbers of people has made many of us isolated in ghettos of strangers, never knowing our neighbors or helping those in need.

Today, it's more important than ever to stay connected to friends and family—to those whom you choose to stay connected to in positive relationships—no matter what.

Stay aware of changing technology. If you are not computer literate, take a class or barter with a friend who can teach you. Do not allow yourself to become marginalized by becoming obsolete. It takes effort. It takes time. You have plenty of time. And we have already discussed the fact that your energy supply can be enhanced by using your head. Keep up with things in your world.

Read about new ideas and taste them in your life. Chew on them. Digest them. They are not fattening. And it is so good for you to vary your diet of thoughts and beliefs. We must change, or we will wither. We must grow, or we will shrink. We have minds with unbelievable powers of expansion.

Use *yours*.

Chapter 8

Take a Lover!

To think of virginity as a virtue—and not a barrier that separates ignorance from knowledge—is an infantile superstition.

—Voltaire

Why wait? Take a cookie when it is passed. Find true love later.

Don't pass up a tasty offering while waiting for a bigger treat.

Take a lover now.

Even if you think this chapter is not for you, why not read it, anyway? You may learn something. You may need it later. Life has a way of testing our resolve sometimes when we think a part of our lives is over. A lover now can hold a place for a more lasting and serious relationship in the future. Or he may simply be entertaining for a woman who is no longer interested in a more serious partner, but whose body still craves sexual release.

Do understand that I am not belittling true love. Sometimes

we have to wait for it to appear. That does not mean we have to wait in celibacy. Ways exist that can alleviate our body's need for sexual release. The saying, "Use it or lose it," fits this situation.

I really believe this. Doctors believe it is healthier to make love than to be celibate. Recently I heard of a study on men that said they should ejaculate three times a week for optimum prostate health. Let's help those men out!

I hate it when I hear a woman speaking of her physical love life as though it's in the past. I hear this from time to time, "That part of my life is over." When I hear it, I always react by saying, "How do you know?" When a woman tells me she simply does not feel desire anymore, I tell her that she simply has not found the right man to make it happen.

BEGIN WITH YOUR IMAGINATION

Even if you do not have a specific person in mind, allow yourself to speculate. Imagine a lover just as you would like him to be. It is more likely that you will find him if you know what you are looking for. But be careful that you do not set yourself up for failure by having impossibly high standards. If you are over 60, for instance, you might be disappointed if your ideal lover is 20. Be realistic, but do not hesitate to dream. And let the dreams be big ones. Do not limit the Universe by only wishing for tiny, obtainable goals.

And do not use the excuse of age as a reason for not finding a man to adore you. As I mentioned before, my own mother married her second husband at the age of 81. At the wedding we all noticed how much her new husband was attracted to her physically. I know of many women in their 80s and 90s who have found a friend after a beloved spouse had passed on before.

This is not disloyalty. It is life. As I have said repeatedly, you

do not know how many more years you may live. It may be a
lot longer than you think. So, make plans. Do not waste your
mature inspired years thinking your sex life is over. You may cut
yourself off from some other partner who is longing for some
romance.

Some women turn to other women during these later years
and find love among their own sex. This may be more and more
prevalent as we age more healthily. We may be healthier than
our fathers and mothers, and yet the men still seem to last a
shorter time than females do.

Whatever outlet you choose will be healthy for you. It is
so true that you must use your talents and your body and your
emotions, to keep them limber and ready to deal with whatever
comes. Keep the sexual part of your body in mind every day.
You can play by yourself until you find a partner, but just do
not put that part of your life behind you completely. It is just as
important as any other component.

A lover is a wonderful addition to your life. In fact, I believe
that it is possible to find a lover without finding true love. It is
sometimes fun to begin a relationship just for recreation. You
do not have to be so in love that you want to make a perma-
nent commitment in order to just enjoy a man. Go ahead and
contemplate a lover that would *never* make a good husband.
Perhaps someone much younger or older takes your fancy. Or
perhaps it is someone who could never support you as a wife
but who makes your body purr with delight.

I believe in physical love. This directive may not have appeal
for everyone, but I urge you to consider it. Even if your body
seems no longer capable of physical release, you might surprise
yourself if you find a person to whom you feel attracted and
let things go along as nature would have them. Not all physical pleasure lies in orgasm. The closeness and trust afforded by

intimacy interact with your mind and body to create health and a feeling of completeness.

Go for it.

Our system of moral judgment is much reduced compared to "the old days." Take advantage of this. I am not suggesting that you do anything that makes you uncomfortable. However, if you just bend the rules a little, keeping those that you think are important and allow yourself some leeway, you may surprise yourself with a lover who helps you get to the next level.

Making love burns calories and makes your heart sing.

TAKE STEPS

It is not so hard as you think to find a lover. There are men out there saying "if only I could find a "f**k-buddy," to use a term popular among young, single women these days. It is a shame that we cannot wear a sign advertising our status: *No Vacancy* or, conversely....*VACANCY.*

Because of the Internet, we now all have the means for finding exactly what we need. I'm repeating myself, I know, but I'm doing so in an attempt to get though your resistance to idea of Internet dating. Maybe by the third or fourth time you hear it, you'll start to open up to the idea. I'm only trying to get you to consider it, to try it out.

So consider. And for those who already got the message and are in action, congratulations!

There are hundreds (if not thousands) of dating sites that bring people together. Even the "rooms" at AOL can be conducive to finding a friend. Of course you might find someone who is far away. It may be that you will only want a "cyber" friend. That is easy. If you wish to find someone in the same town or nearby, that is easy enough to select also. *Craig's List* is one of the best sites. It is free, and it is diverse. You can ask for exactly what you want there. Simply plug in the nearest city and list your criteria for a partner.

There are plenty of other sites. Again, *GoCougar.com* is a site where older women can connect with younger men. All of these websites are safe if you use your head. Do not give out personal information or meet a stranger in a place where you are not comfortable and within earshot of other people. As I mentioned earlier, *eHarmony.com* is one of the very safest because there are so many layers of protection between you and the men you may speak to. It can take a fair amount of time before you actually get to phone conversations because of all of the different levels and test questions on that site.

New sites crop up all the time. You may be able to find one for your school or your town or your region. You are almost certainly going to find a site that caters to your religion or your political party. There are also sites for every imaginable quirky desire. Use caution, but enjoy the huge variety available to you.

ABOUT THE LOVER

Try to stay clear of married men. But if you must, find one who is not having sex with his wife. There seem to be quite a number of those. I am not certain of the percentage, but it is more than one would like to think about.

Married men are not a good idea for so many reasons besides the normal ones of morality. They simply cannot give you enough attention. Their loyalties and their time and resources are tied up. They may call you by their wife's name or vice versa, which is much worse. The consequences are desperately serious. Do not do it.

There are actually many single men out there. Meeting them is tricky but they do surface from time to time. The good ones do not know how to meet women. They are lost. The men who are smooth and know all the moves and seem completely at ease are most likely "snakes." They have been at this game for a while and know the ropes. They are *not* interested in finding a solid relationship, but rather are interested in seeing how many skirts they can collect, so to speak. This is not a good basis for taking them as a lover.

Shy and lazy men sometimes make the best catches because they do not come with entanglements and baggage. They are ill at ease and frightened of making a mistake. They feel foolish making small talk. They are not practiced in the art of seduction. But they do want to have sex with you. That is important because, of course, there are some men out there who do *not*.

There is a large gay community. It seems to me that it is getting larger. But maybe that is an illusion brought on by the fact that finally these men can speak openly and live openly with their partners. You do not want one of them. Having a gay friend is fine. However, what this chapter is all about is finding men who will be fun for you to fall in love with. Do not fall in love with a gay man. It will lead to heartache for you both. Gay men do not need love affairs with women. Do not start thinking you will change him. You will not.

Start from the position that there are millions of single men. There are, but some of them are awfully young for you. Now don't be shocked at what I am about to say. Age is a very misunderstood thing. Women and men of varying ages can have wonderful relationships as lovers. Look all around you. Do not rule anyone out due to age except the under-age ones. And you can keep an eye on them, too, because one day they will grow up enough to be legal. (Just teasing here, but I believe you get my drift.)

ABOUT YOUR BODY

Keep working on your body all the time but do not think in terms of "when I get my figure back," or some other limit on when and with whom you may find a relationship. You deserve to be loved exactly as you are.

And when you meet the right person that is exactly what will happen. You do not have to be perfect. Your figure does not have to be perfect, either. Just relax about that. But keep eating better and better and exercising so that you will stay healthy and "juicy." That is what is important. It is hard to attract someone when you are ill or even just under the weather. Especially if that "weather" is of your own making. That is why I want you to read the section on staying healthy in Chapter 5, *Get Healthy!* of this book. It is a must. Without your health, all the rest is wasted.

I hasten to add that I know of people with true physical disabilities who are leading productive and happy love lives as well as other areas of their lives. I believe that this is almost solely due to attitude.

Ask yourself: Do you believe you are "worth it" in spite of problems? Do you believe that you are valuable and worthy? If you do, so will someone else.

One woman with whom I spoke has had extensive radiation for cervical cancer. Her body is limited in its sexual capacity. But she believes that men and women need to be intimate if they are in a relationship. She is prepared to ease her husband's sexual needs in a loving and giving way and, in return, he is tender with her needs as well.

Other women—women who have undergone hysterectomies—sometimes say they are affected sexually by the operation. Many feel that they are more sexy without their plumbing. I have always wondered about that. I will continue to try to discover why some women seem pleased and others devastated by this all-too-common operation. I do not want to make anyone feel guilty for having had this surgery. However, it is estimated that it is the most over-performed surgery in the USA. Or it was until recently, when the C-section rate for birthing babies is taking over as the most-performed operation of an unnecessary nature in the country. I would like to see the numbers of both of these operations take a steep dive.

Women tend to be too trusting of what their doctors say. They do not research the diagnosis. They do not go to a different medical practice for a second opinion. Why don't they? One reason is that women do not speak up about their pain when they are victims of unnecessary surgery. Because of this, their sisters go willingly under the knife. It is an epidemic that is still waiting for an exposé to make enough people angry. When that happens there will be constraints put on doctors to stop all this cutting and try something new.

ADAM AND EVE, BUT MOSTLY EVE

I have a theory about what women want. It is very unconventional and a bit scandalous, and some would even say sacrilegious. It concerns the Adam and Eve story of Creation.

In the Book of Genesis, God told Adam not to eat of the fruit of the tree of knowledge. He told Eve as well to obey his command. But what was God thinking? Did he really mean it? As a parent, didn't you prohibit your child from doing something—like riding a bike in the street—because you felt that child was not yet ready to do it? You did not forbid it forever in your own mind. It was a temporary directive.

God, acting in place as the ultimate parent, may have been doing the same thing when he gave his directive to Adam and Eve. What if he only meant to protect them, expecting later they would become mature and be able to handle more? Knowing they would grow and mature, what if God were simply test-ing Adam and Eve?

I believe that God must have been very proud of Eve, even as he punished them. She had the guts to think for herself. She had the courage to disobey. She even admitted that she did it. She was curious, and she caused her safe harbor to disappear.

But in place of that safe harbor were infinite possibilities. A whole new world! The fruits of her labors, not God's.

Along with this was Adam's response. He blamed his own eating of the apple on the woman. He did not take responsibility for disobeying. He acted like a coward and a heel. Perhaps Eve was disappointed in him. Perhaps Eve did not want Adam at all. Perhaps Eve really wanted God. Perhaps our troubles started there, but not in the way that the church treats it now.

Maybe all of us women want God. We are not satisfied by mortal man. We secretly long for God. Not to pray, but to wed us and protect us and love us forever. If this shocks you, please get over it and think about it for a minute. There is some deep truth here. We do expect a great deal from our men. Suppose we are always searching not for our other half, as the Greeks be-lieved, but for God Himself as our completion and fulfillment. (Or in the case of men, for the Goddess.)

What we want is supernatural and therefore unattainable.

No wonder we are often frustrated by love.

On the other hand, do you know what you are looking for? Do you have an ideal man in mind? Do you know what he should be like? Do you have a physical ideal? What about his mind? Do you have a level of income or a type of job in mind when you think of your future mate? If you cannot readily an-swer these questions, I have a task for you.

WRITE IT DOWN

Write it down. Write it down in detail. Do it now. Or, if you simply cannot find the time right away, then make an appointment with yourself to do it later. Do not delay. Again, I am repeating myself, but only because many of you did not do this the first time I mentioned it. If you did, I applaud you. You are that much closer to your goals being realized. But for those of you who didn't, the opportunity is coming around again. For your own sake, please follow my suggestion and *write it down!*

This is how our minds help us achieve our goals. First, we visualize them. Then we make an action plan for achieving them. Then we must take some kind of action. Then we wait for the Universe to do its work.

Once you've written it down, make an action plan. You must be sure that the action plan is feasible. You must actually do something about it. You must put yourself in the path of what you desire. For instance, if your job is as a lowly assistant in a low-level industry, and your ideal mate is a CEO of a major company, you must make some very great changes in your life to put yourself in his path. Be realistic, but do not hesitate to dream big. Just be sure to write it all down and visualize what you have dreamed up.

This powerful tool goes unused by so many women and men. Yet any good athletic coach will tell you that your mental game is as important as the physical. This is most often achieved through visualization. In order to know what to visualize, write it down. This helps you to understand and refine what you truly desire. It is so simple. It is so effective. Why is it so hard for so many of us to sit down and do this? Perhaps we fear our own power. Perhaps we instinctively know that if we know what we want, we may achieve it. It is a frightening thought. "Be careful what you wish for," because you may indeed be granted your wish.

So many times in my life, I have found myself doing something that was a dream of mine at some earlier date. It has happened so many times that I have developed a healthy fear of my own wishes, my own power to manifest them. Perhaps it is a higher power who helps us achieve our longed-for goals. Perhaps it is our own energy or that of the Universe.

Never mind what makes it happen. Just believe that it does happen.

More important is the necessity of your knowing what it is that you truly want. Do not waste the power on things that make you unhealthy. Do not wish for fatty food or gambling wins or unlimited cocktails. These kinds of things represent short-term wishing, an idle practice. Be judicious in your choices. Our own wishes are among the most powerful forces in our lives. Do not abuse them.

Never think that your dreams are impossible. There are too many examples to list here of women (and men) who wished for something that seemed too much to ask for at the time they wished it, but nevertheless, it was theirs. These stories are varied. There is no set method for attaining wishes. However, there are some rules that make it easier.

Write it down. Are you surprised? How many times do I have to say this? Take a pen and paper or type on your computer, but make it tangible. Make it legible. Make it readable. But do it now.

DEAL WITH YOUR FEARS

The other night, I was speaking with a woman about taking a lover. She was more or less horrified that I would speak of this at a cocktail party. But why not? It seemed like a perfectly good place to me. She was curious but very skeptical. When I told her that the Internet was an excellent place to find a man, she was genuinely frightened.

The most frequently mentioned horror story is the mass murderer Ted Bundy. All sorts of women say that they heard he was a charmer. That may be so. I never met Ted Bundy.

I still contend that the Internet allows a distance and anonymity that would be impossible in a bar or any other place where you are sitting across from a person who is a stranger to you. Online, you can wait to use your real name until you feel completely safe. You do not have to give out any information that could lead a man to you. You may find it reassuring to know that most men are frightened, too. They have no idea what they are getting. Women lie. Women tell all sorts of stories about their looks. No wonder the men are gun shy.

Men lie about their height and their weight and their ages and their income. But it is all because they want desperately to find someone who will "fill in the gap," as Rocky said in the first film of that name.

Women want this, too. But they want someone who is financially stable and not a drunk. They want a man who will listen to them, a man who will cuddle in bed at night or spoon on the sofa on a rainy afternoon instead of staying glued to the game. This man will look like a hero to many women.

Back to the fear of contacting a pervert or sex fiend online. There are many perfectly normal (whatever that means) men out there. They all have faults. We do, too. Why is it that women cannot seem to deal with the reality of men? They have calluses on their toes. They love violent sports more than we do. They like to lie around and do nothing sometimes. They do not find it interesting to dissect each thought as it passes through their minds. They are men.

Get over it.

Genetically, men and women have different jobs. Ours includes gathering (i.e., shopping). It also often includes the meeting and greeting of friends as well as strangers. So if we are going to meet *men*, we must take the initiative. We must be brave enough to experiment with online meetings. It is so easy. It is private. It is less embarrassing than hanging out at singles bars or even on a cruise where everyone suspects you are there for the "trolling."

The woman I was speaking with (remember the cocktail party I just spoke of?) was married, so it doesn't really count. Nevertheless, she was looking at me as if I were completely crazy. I really do believe in online meeting. So many people have met their mates there. I think it is one of the best ways to equalize the playing field. You cannot bring your normal visual prejudices right away to the relationship. You have to base your desire to follow up with a man on the letters you receive from him.

You can tell if someone is educated by the words he uses or spelling or syntax he uses. Spelling is only a partial test as there are many of us who are "spelling impaired," and yet can string words together in an amusing way. You can tell if a man is funny or if he is dull or "thick" intellectually. Humor comes through, as does irony. It is no different than any author being able to express a thought. If you are "instant-messaging" someone, you can tell by the speed with which he answers whether he is quick on the uptake or not.

I love meeting people this way. It is so friendly. It is so fast and so convenient because I may be sitting at my computer in my most comfortable nightie with a cup of coffee by my elbow. The fire may be glowing beneath my mantel and smooth sounds coming from my iPod as it plays cradled in its speakers. It can be the most relaxed time of day. There is no pressure to wear the correct thing or outshine anyone else. It is you and your email or Instant Message partner. If there are distractions you can ignore them or come back to this later. Besides that, there is the time element. You are not in a rush. There is no beginning or end to the conversation. You may take a day or weeks to decide you want to move on to the phone.

When you do decide to call a man, be sure to ask him for his number and then block your own for privacy. That way you are perfectly safe from predators, in case you have been misled by the man. You can keep your anonymity as long as you wish, but I suggest that you decide fairly soon whether you trust this man. Do not let things drag on without establishing who you both are. If he is not forthcoming about his job or marital status or place of residence, then just move on. You do not want to become embroiled with a man whom you cannot trust.

Some women seem to feel that it is okay for a man to put them off and keep part of himself private. That is true, up to a point. But if a man whom you are seeing will not let you inside his apartment or house, that is a very large red flag. Do not expect to keep that relationship. That man is hiding something from you even if it is not specifically something in his rooms. You deserve a man who is open and honest. You do not want a man who keeps parts of his life secret. Privacy is one thing; secrecy is another thing entirely.

Always have enough self respect to understand that you are worth knowing. You are worth his honesty. You are worth everyone's honesty. Do not allow yourself to be lied to. Do you feel that you must be careful to be a certain way so that you won't lose that man? If so, he is *not* the man for you.

You deserve to be loved exactly the way you are. You are perfect as you are. You are the sum of all the things you have done all of your life. You have nothing to apologize for. Some man will find you to be the answer to his dreams. If there is one thing I have learned from all the women I have interviewed it is that there is someone for *everyone*.

It is the most amazing thing. Nature or our Guardian Angels or some Force we do not understand has a plan for how it will all work out, and it does. First you have to want it. That is why I keep saying, *write down what it is that you want.* You must visualize it. Even if you don't really see a "picture," it is the act of formalizing your desires by listing them on paper or drawing a picture, if you are able, or recording it on tape or CD.

Enjoy the Search

Finding a lover is easier than you think. You must be careful, of course. But if you will expand your parameters and remember that we are only speaking of a "lover"--not a husband--then you may find release and extraordinary fun in surprising places. You can ask all the questions you want. You can ask for a medical release. You can certainly ask for safe sex, as well. Do be careful of your body and "vet" any man you are considering being intimate with. Of course you could be fooled, so be careful.

Do not take this part lightly. It is, after all, life-and-death serious. Decreasing your risk of encountering surprise diseases is one reason I recommend finding a long-term partner as a lover, rather than a one-night stand. This is definitely possible. You just have to know what you are looking for. There are a lot of nice men out there who simply cannot seem to find regular sex from a loving woman. I am not sure why that is. I believe that subject is a whole different book.

It seems impossible that men are having trouble when women are so sure that there are no men around. There are men around, but some of them rush from one committed relationship to another. Women do this, too. It is the easy way out, if you ask me. You never have the fun of playing the field. You just jump full-tilt into a new relationship. How do you know that it won't be worse than the one you just left? Give yourself some time.

It is nice to have a lover. It is also nice to be alone for awhile and just find yourself. When you have had time to decompress and discover what it is that you really think would be fun, then set out to find it. By that, I mean "online" at first. Because I find this such an excellent way to fine-tune what you are looking for, I recommend that you learn to work a computer if you are not already computer-savvy.

Even if you don't need it for finding a lover, a computer will help you in the 21st century. We are all going to have to know how to use the infernal machines; otherwise we will be like those who were afraid of horseless carriages in the early part of the last century. You don't want to be one of those, do you?

Back to the Internet and my suggestions for what to do there. Follow the directions.

MEETING AND BEYOND

Suppose you have found a man who seems interesting and interested. What do you do now? Well, I am assuming you have begun speaking on the phone. If he sounds safe and sexy at the same time, he may be worth meeting. Be careful to find a place that you know about. Find a spot where parking is easy. Make sure it is lit at night and well traveled.

Personally, I like to meet for coffee on a Saturday morning or lunch in a shopping center. Drinks are okay, but be careful not to have too many. Some men become more aggressive at night and may think they can get away with being forcefully insistent with you in a darkened parking lot. Just be aware. Do not take stupid chances.

Do not meet at all until you feel 100 percent comfortable with the man. It is just not worth the risk otherwise, and there are so many men waiting to meet you. Do not ever think there is only one.

Okay, so you have met. You like him. He likes you. Now what? Well, now the fun begins. Do you feel that you need to date? That is not necessary if all you seek is a lover. A lover can be secret. You can have a relationship that is totally incongruous but highly sexual and loads of fun. A lover is for fun. We are not talking about a marriage partner—though, of course, that could develop.

When I was a teenager, my father told me never to date a man I could not imagine marrying. I believed him. But that advice was based on his fear that something like a pregnancy might occur. Now, with birth control, fathers can relax a bit more. And for us women who are over 50, the chances of pregnancy are slim. After menopause we are safe from that concern.

I believe that you can find a lover who will make you smile, make you laugh, make your body sing. This man can be someone you would never consider marrying, and that is okay. It is exciting to seek outside of your normal group. Ethnicity and religion and financial security make little difference in a lover. You can take chances. You can learn about other cultures. You can do what you please.

So what do you do when you are alone with this person? That will depend on both of you. But it is important for you to realize that this is going to be fun. Do not let embarrassment spoil your meeting. Toss out old ideas of what is proper. Pick clothes to wear that are comfortable and come off easily. Be sexy. Pantyhose are a nuisance. Try thigh highs. Wear a dress or a skirt. Skip the underwear. Or find some that is sexy and flattering and perhaps figure-enhancing.

One final word: About your body, relax. Men are very visual, that is true. However, they are seriously excited by a woman's available body no matter whether it is perfect or not. You must get over all the worries about whether you look like a movie star or not. You probably do not. Even movie stars don't really look like they seem to on film. No one does.

The most exciting thing to a man is *enthusiasm*. It you want him, truly want him, then you will be beautiful in his eyes. If you kiss him with gusto, he will respond with the same. Nothing is quite so exciting as meeting a man whom you know you are going to make love to for the first time. He will also feel this. There is magic in it. Stop worrying and enjoy the moment.

You are grown up. You can speak up for yourself and tell the man if anything is making you uncomfortable. Be sure you do this. Don't just lie there and endure. Be a participant in your lovemaking. Say what you like and say what you do not like. Give him encouragement when he is pleasing you. Thank him. Smile. Snuggle against him. Tell him what turns you on and what you like about him and what he is doing. Be enthusiastic. Be brave about showing your pleasure. Do not stay silent. Men like feedback, especially positive feedback.

Enjoy!

CHAPTER 9

BE GRATEFUL

Don't wait for a light to appear at the end of the tunnel,
stride down there ...and light the bloody thing yourself.
—SARA HENDERSON, WRITER

Gratitude bathes us in light and hope. It works as a beauty cream, an elixir for health and energy. No price tag or limited quantities keep us from enjoying as much gratitude as we want. This is probably the most important emotion of all. It makes us happy to be grateful, and it makes us attractive to others.

Want to cultivate more of this beauty-enhancer? See everything as a gift. Even things that seem to be stumbling blocks or downright disasters can be the beginning of something wonderful. Just be sure that you understand this: your attitude is in your own hands. You can decide whether to look at something as a good thing about to happen or a disaster that will never be forgotten.

IT'S ALL A GIFT

This day is a gift. Every day is.

I walk three miles every day. It keeps me fit physically, but the true benefits are psychological. Every day on my walk, I feel grateful for my legs for carrying me. I feel grateful for the day. I feel grateful for the many gifts I have been given in allowing me the beautiful views that I see every day. I am speaking of the trees and the birds and the greenery. Even if it is raining, I must walk. I have a small dog who demands it even when I am tired or busy or out of sorts. By the time I am finished with my walk, I feel better. It energizes me.

Be grateful for your legs and the ability to walk. Some cannot. When I go for my walks or when I am in an exercise class, I always find myself being grateful for the fact that I am mobile. I often say a little prayer of thanks for my legs. I have been doing this ever since I was a young girl. There are things that I wish for about my body, like the ability I once had to eat whatever I wished and not gain weight. There are shapes that I would prefer to my own. But, by and large, I am happy for my body to be mine and in good working order. Your body is a huge gift. Appreciate it.

Your parents are a gift, whether they are or were good or bad parents. Someone to whom I spoke recently said that forgiving her parents was one of the most important things for her to have done. Have you done so? Parents rarely perform perfectly. All of us who are parents should understand this. And if you do not have children but are an adult, it is time for you to know this. Parents often fail even when they are trying their hardest to succeed, and yes, some parents are just plain rotten. Either way, it is not anything you can change. What you can change is your attitude about your childhood.

Of course, the problem with parents can continue your whole life. Even after they are gone, the residual effects remain if we allow them to. But we can change our minds. You can change *your* mind. Focus on the good and, if there was no good, then focus on getting over it.

Even a terrible childhood can be a gift. If nothing else it can be a lesson in what not to do. My mother was a stickler for "everything in its place," and sadly, as a result, I tend to do the opposite. I'm not sure why her telling me that there should be a place for everything did not seem to make me want to emulate her. But I have a sloppy streak that gets me in trouble all the time. At least I recognize the problem, and I seriously try to remedy it.

Many people have awful things to forget or overcome. But they manage it. You can, too. No whining allowed here.

Get busy trying to stop negative thoughts from overtaking you in your day-to-day living. I believe that you must allow these thoughts to pass on through and keep going. If you try to deny them they take a stronger hold on your psyche. So acknowledge them, but let them go. I tie a mental hot air balloon to these thoughts and let them fly away. I have been doing this for years, and new ones keep surfacing. That is okay. I just keep sending them off into the stratosphere and go forward with less baggage. It works.

Be grateful for every setback, because setbacks can be windows of opportunity to look through and see things you never imagined. There is a Country Western song that has the lyrics: "Thank God for unanswered prayers." I have always smiled when I heard those words. So many times in my life, I have prayed to have something or to keep something that really would not have been good for me. It is so hard to see this at the time you are praying for it, but years later it becomes much clearer.

Many times I believe we are led to find new avenues when the ones we think we want to follow are forbidden to us. Do not let disappointments stop you from seeking your goals. And if you are stymied over and over when seeking something illusive, it may be that that is not the goal you were meant to achieve.

Try another. There are so many different approaches to things. Life is not nearly as simple as we believed when we were children. Search out the things that are easy for you to do and enjoy them. Do those things well and plan for more difficult tasks and goals for the future.

I am not advocating taking the easy road at all times. Not in the least. But sometimes, while following the path that is easy for us, we discover side trips that bring us great joy. I do not believe that life is meant to be difficult all the time.

Gratitude is more contagious than fear or anger. Go and spread it. Gratitude is fun. Like smiling. I believe that feeling gratitude changes the physiology of the brain. It is almost impossible to feel sorry for yourself while feeling grateful. The two simply do not go together at all.

It is so easy to begin. Look around you. Is it daytime? What do you see? Do you see the sun beaming down on the world giving of its golden light, its warmth and health supporting Vitamin D?

Is it night? Is there a velvety darkness folding you into its protective cover? Do you know that soon you will lay your head on your pillow and find release in slumber? Or are you about to go out and see friends for the evening? Do you savor the vision of streetlights bathing the streets and sidewalks with their radiant glow?

Either day or night, there is much to be grateful for just knowing what time of day it is. Hoping you would like to go further, I always feel grateful for my health. Sometimes I remember what it feels like to have a horrible cold. It feels dreadful. But if I do not have one (and I almost never do any more) I am grateful for feeling un-stuffy and for having a clear sense of smell and taste and feeling well in general. This is easy, too. Often I feel that we are so wrapped up in needs and wants and disappointments that we overlook the positives in our lives this instant. If we take the time to notice, we will feel instantly better. And besides that, I believe we build up some imaginary credit with the Universe for noticing our bounty.

From Fear to Gratitude

Riding horses has been my principle sport since I was a little girl. I love it; I have enjoyed it all of my adult life. When I was 42, I had a bad fall from my horse. I broke some vertebrae in my back while fox hunting in the beautiful Virginia countryside. It scared me badly. I feared paralysis more than anything, and breaking bones in one's back is frightening. Though I rode again that year after my bones healed, my "nerve" was still injured. I began to be fearful when riding to hounds, and I knew that it was no longer safe for me to do it. Riders who have lost their nerve prove to be dangerous to others, as well as themselves. So I stopped hunting.

Several years passed. I never missed hunting a bit. But one spring day, I decided to hack to a hunt meet that was near my farm. I was riding a good horse which my husband and daughters rode often and hunted regularly. I never meant to actually go hunting that day. I simply wanted to ride for the pleasure of it. I had not jumped a fence in years.

We set out from the meet at a walk and I just followed along, talking to a woman whom I knew well and liked a lot, June Rusham. After a few minutes we started a slow trot, and I just jogged along chatting mindlessly as I enjoyed the blue sky and early spring sights and sounds. All of a sudden, I realized that horses somewhere in front of where I was riding were jumping a jump. I said to my friend, "Oh Dear! I am not sure that I want to jump anything."

June replied, "Well, it is a very friendly little fence." I looked ahead and I could see that what they were jumping was a small stone wall with a wooden rail placed horizontally over it. Probably not much higher than two and a half feet, it posed not the slightest trouble to the big, fit, experienced horse that I was riding. And I suddenly realized that the horse had to do the jumping, not me. That horse had hunted regularly all year. All I had to do was hang on.

I gave the horse his head and jumped easily over the wall. We began to trot faster, and a second small wall came into view. This time I barely gave it a thought. It felt wonderful to sail over it on the safe and experienced animal under me.

Then, as we began to canter, my husband rode up to me saying, "There is a rather large stone wall up ahead. Do you want to come with me to find a way around it?"

I answered as I cantered closer, "How big?" And even as the words were spoken, I could see the wall ahead of me. It was a fairly high wall, and there was no protecting rail across it, making it a lot more dangerous to jump. But at the same time, I remembered that I had jumped this same wall many times in years past. My horse had jumped it much more recently. And even as part of me felt a residual fear, the rest of me went forward at a collected canter and simply sat calmly as my horse cleared the wall. As I became airborne, I could feel a smile completely and exultantly cover my face. I was ecstatic. I had conquered my fear, and I was having fun.

The interesting part of this story stems from the words that my friend said to me when I contemplated jumping the first small wall. She did *not* say, "Oh, you had better not jump it!" Nor did she try to shame me by saying, "Oh, of course you should jump it." She merely said, "It is a very friendly fence," and let me figure out the rest.

For many years after that, I thanked my friend June every time I saw her out hunting. If it were not for her tact, I might never have found that joy and freedom and confidence again.

It is so important to be careful not to destroy someone's confidence when they are taking a chance. It is vital to think about the consequences when you criticize or chastise someone who tries to work themselves out of their comfort zone. We all need friends like June Rusham.

PRAY

Even if you are not religious, is there anyone out there who does not have a spiritual facet to his or her character? I defy you to see a beautiful sunset or sunrise or thunderstorm or rainbow without feeling awe and, in many cases, gratitude. Enjoy the feeling. It will heal you.

It is true that religion and its teachings are often a problem when it comes to a better life. So many of our Western religions act as though happiness were a sin. Eastern religions are different. The Dalai Lama tells us that happiness is our right. He says the art of being happy is a learned skill which we may all cultivate. It is not all that difficult, in fact.

First we must pare away our resentments. We must forget anger as a cure for anything. There is not a shred of good in it. We have the choice to be or do or feel these things. We may feel terrible, but we can choose to let go of anger. This is one of life's lessons that we are more likely to understand after the age of 50. It is a hard lesson for many of us. But when we learn how much control we have over our own emotions we suddenly find life much more fun and a lot less "random."

Gratitude is healthy. It makes tension evaporate. It makes days pleasant and work loads lighter. It is contagious. We have so much to be grateful about.

One is the fact that it is so hard to find a man who is "the one." This is cause for much complaining among women. I always laugh when I hear this particular complaint. I think: What a gift it is that it is so hard! Can you imagine what a difficult life you would lead if you were attracted to a new man every week, every month? Suppose you married one and then within weeks saw another whom you liked as well.

It is a gift to us that we only find a very few people in our whole lives whom we think of as "the One." It may be a childhood love, maybe a first adult relationship that lasted for years, maybe your husband. But then life has a way of shaking us up and changing our plans. Either because of death, illness of a debilitating type or divorce, many women find themselves single again and available, whether they ever thought they would want such a thing or not.

These women can be very picky about men. There are so many rules now for men, I often feel sorry for them. Everyone complains about the quality of men. They say that they are *all* cretins. They are not attracted to them, they are fat or surly, or have funny nose hair.

But this is also a blessing! What if every man attracted us? We would spend our lives in perpetual frustration and despair. In fact. I think that what happens with some men is that their sex drive is so highly developed that they are constantly aroused by all sorts of women. Perhaps this is a stereotype, but they say Italian men are this way. It can be a problem. Most women are not so easily distracted by a new man.

That it is hard to find a match, that so many men do not attract us, is a blessing. Be thankful that you cannot just jump from one relationship to another. It is much healthier to spend some time alone and find out who you are before attaching yourself to another man. This seems hard to do, but it is so very much a fact.

I know women love to have the next mate picked out before they leave the first one. This has been a universal desire. Fear is the reason. Many women have low self-esteem and feel useless and old when they are just beginning to hit their stride. It is really important to understand today just how much things have changed.

We women are no longer finished at 40, 50, 60, 70, or even 80. We may have years to live and many possibilities and good health to see us through. This is completely new. Fifty years ago, widows of age 50 rarely married again. These women often moved in with their grown children. Now a 50-year-old single woman might go back to college, as I did, or start a new job or career, might marry again, or take a lover, almost certainly would live on her own. She probably is self-supporting. She can take care of herself.

All of these are changes we can be grateful for. We are living in a wonderful time.

Chapter 10

Become Wise

Most powerful is he who has himself in his own power.
—Seneca, Roman Philosopher and Statesman

Wisdom—yours or anyone's—is a quality that draws people and events to you.

Use it.

Dwelling on the past will not attract people and events. You cannot do anything to change the past. Let that desire go. You have much more power than you know to direct what happens to you in the future.

If you look back with clear eyes, you will find there all sorts of lessons and directions that can help you avoid mistakes in the future. I know I always say, "Don't look back!" But there are times when looking back is helpful.

Learning from your past mistakes grants you wisdom. If something happens to you that you do not think you can handle, chances are it resembles something you have *already* handled in the past. Use this knowledge and apply it to your current circumstances. When you learn from your mistakes of the past, at least they will have served a purpose.

WISDOM: A GIFT AND SKILL

Wisdom is the gift we receive for growing older. Some of us receive more of it than others, it seems.

I believe that wisdom is also a learned skill. Women who are dealing with a crisis often acquire it. This skill can be forming somewhere deep inside you without your knowledge. Then it bursts forth when you need it to solve or resolve a situation or deal with desperate feelings of all sorts.

Once we discover that our attitude guides all of our results, we can learn that a good attitude cancels bad luck. This really works. It reminds me of the ancient Chinese proverb about a farmer whose horse ran away. His neighbors said to him, "Bad Luck!" But the farmer said, "Maybe." Later the horse returned bringing two new mares with it. The neighbors, seeing this said, "What good luck!" But the farmer said, "Maybe." The man's son tried riding one of the new wild horses and had a fall, breaking his leg. The neighbors said, "What bad luck!" I know that you will not be surprised to hear that the man said, "Maybe." A couple of days later, the military came through, conscripting young men for the army. Seeing that the farmer's son had a broken leg, they left him alone and went off with the sons of many of the neighbors. The neighbors said to the farmer, "What good luck you have!" and, of course, the farmer said, "Maybe."

I believe that belief is the most important quality in achieving our goals. This is not my idea. It is the most ancient idea of any self-help method. I believe that even before written words were put in stone or on clay tablets, the "enlightened" understood about belief. *What you believe determines what will happen.* It is so powerful, you must be careful with this ability. It can backfire. But it can also make your life a constant flow of ideas and realities that are exactly what you wish for or imagine.

In order to achieve your most heartfelt desires, surround yourself with the feelings of joy or contentment that achieving your desire would give you if you already had them. There are a lot of people talking about this sort of thing now. Experience what you want as if it were real, and it will become real.

The motivational speaker Wallace D. Wattles said: "If you have not consciously made the decision to be rich, excellent, and healthy, then you have unconsciously made the decision to be poor, mediocre, and unhealthy." I agree 100 percent. The future is in your hands.

You are not a victim.

You are the captain of your own ship. Steer it well. Have confidence in your ability to go in the direction you want to. Never mind where you have been or what happened to you there. You can redirect yourself and your future at any time.

You have the tools to be happy and content. Even if your health deteriorates as you find yourself in your 90s or 100s, you can enjoy music, reading or audio books, art and simply watching nature at its work. Feelings of love and gratitude breed more of the same. They change your brain chemistry while they make you feel wonderful.

By now you know that negative thoughts can harm you. Do you know that they can simply make you feel bad? Let your thoughts be happy ones. Encourage more of them just as you might plant a garden. Find new varieties of happiness to recall. The more you focus on happiness, the more of it you will find. Focus and belief, these are all you need. Even if you are alone you can be content. If there is interaction with another human being, let it be positive.

When you were young, I bet you spent hours reliving mistakes that you made and regretting things that are past. How much time do you suppose you should devote to this in the future? That is right....*zero.*

You have learned that it is futile to mull over the past. The future is bright. Even if you are near death, it is bright. For after you pass over to the other side, you will find a new reality. I believe this is going to be a positive experience for us. Perhaps that belief is instrumental in my overall happiness.

Standard religion doesn't always support such a belief. If you have lived your life in fear of a vengeful God, you may fear death and retribution. Fear of going to Hell has brought forth many a deathbed confession. But what about concentrating on a loving God? No matter what your religion, I believe by the time you reach an advanced age, you know that God is great and kind. Of course, people die and awful things happen to some of us, while others feel guilty for escaping similar fates. But it is all part of a pattern that we cannot understand.

We Are All Connected

We are all one. This idea seems impossible to many, but it is actually backed up by science. More and more, it is accepted that we are all oscillating at a similar frequency, and as energy, share the same vibration. Quantum physics shows us this.

Our children and grandchildren will accept this idea as easily as we do the fact that the earth revolves around the sun. For us, it may seem strange. Yet the sooner we embrace it, the happier and more content we will be. What a relief to understand that even if we hate each other and believe different things, we are all connected to each other. Just like conflicting flora and fauna in the human body, we all inhabit the common space that we call our Universe.

We can fight and feud and hate and struggle, but in the end

we must realize that we are all connected, and there is nothing we can do about it. Once the world decides to accept this fact, things may change somewhat. I doubt this will happen in my lifetime. But sometimes ideas do change almost overnight. There is a tipping point after which everyone suddenly seems to rush out and grasp an idea that most people thought was crazy a short time ago.

I hope that you all will look into this phenomenon, because it will change your life if you can see the truth of it. Once we stop being so parochial, we can expand our consciousness and enjoy the knowledge that an open mind can absorb.

THE WISDOM OF YOUR BODY

Health is essential. I hope you read carefully Chapter 5 on staying healthy. Most important of all is having the wisdom to believe in your own health, that you can be healthy. Next most important is to believe in your ability to know what is best for your body. Yes, you, not your doctor, know what is best for your body and health.

This does *not* mean that all doctors are suspect. But it does mean that many are, so you must be in charge. Do not sit back and wait for your doctor to heal you. You must be proactive. You must see more than one health professional if you are truly ill. Do not let "tunnel vision" kill you, as I have seen it do to so many. Question everything your doctor tells you. Ask questions if you have to be in a hospital or health facility of any kind. If something does not look right, then speak up. Demand answers, and do not worry about being a "pest." It may save your life.

Trust your body, not drugs. Drug companies are definitely suspect. They want you to buy their drugs. They do not want you to stop. They do not want to cure you. They want to sell you more drugs. More and more and more drugs sold to you are more and more profits for the drug companies.

Hey, I am a capitalist. I am not against big business. But I am not going to sit still for it, either. If I see an injustice, I will speak up. And what is happening now with drug companies and doctors is just plain wrong. Drug companies play a large part in educating doctors. So it is no wonder that doctors graduate from medical school with a distorted idea of what good patient care is. They often feel that drugs are better for the patient than herbs or relationships, or music, or just "a tincture of time," which used to be a time-honored way of treating illness. Most of illness cured itself. Now your doctor is more like a drug pusher than a healer.

Don't fall for it. You do not need these drugs. You need to know how your body works. I am not a physician. Nor do I pretend to know all the facets of body-mind medicine. What I do know is that there is another way. Find it. Use it. Save your body from 20th century medicine, which is hopelessly outdated now that we are living in the 21st Century. There are doctors who understand mind-body medicine and acknowledge the wisdom of the body. Find one of them.

Do not ever use a doctor who will not take your concerns, feelings, and emotions seriously. Make sure you can talk about anything and that he or she will listen. Make sure any questions that you ask get answered and, if not, that your doctor is willing to check the research. If your doctor is too busy to give you this information, then he or she is too busy to treat you in any way. Much of healing comes in the time spent talking about treatment. Much of it comes from the feeling between you and any healer to whom you bring your disease.

Dis-ease is exactly what it says. It is a sign that there is something interfering with your *ease*. Listen to what your body is telling you. Do not go outside yourself for information before you have looked inward. Chances are you know what the real problem is. Of course, there are times people would rather die than address the inner problem that causes their illness. If this is the case, there is nothing that I can do. Each of us must understand our own demons. Each of us must follow our own road.

Author Gail Sheehy, in her book *Sex and the Seasoned Woman: Pursuing the Passionate Life*, speaks of the "seasoned woman." I like that description. *Seasoned* like fine wine, like good firewood, like great steaks, we are at our best later in life. Do not fear this time in your life. It is truly the easiest time for you to navigate your path.

With long life comes knowledge and wisdom. It really does appear to us, like a gift from the life we have lived. When things happen that make us sad, we have the wisdom to know that *this too will pass*. We do not need to suffer from any of life's blows, because we know that each of them will pass. This awareness gives us a huge "leg up" in dealing with younger people—our children, grandchildren—who are still so wrapped up in their problems. They feel each one is a once-in-a-lifetime disaster, while we know that nothing is a complete disaster. Each trial that we survive teaches us something of value. If we are lucky, they will teach us many things. Never again will we become vulnerable to the same forces.

Each time we surmount one of life's little trials, we gain strength and wisdom. Be thankful every time life tests you. Each test is worth years of effortless living. No one escapes unscathed. Just remember that you will be okay. You are protected and loved. I know without a doubt that we are not alone and we are protected. Most of the things we fear most never happen to us. Just to be sure, focus on good things, never on bad ones. Do not give attention to those things you do not want.

All the knowledge you have gained in your precious time on earth will help you in these later years. You reap the benefits of all the time you have spent putting out fires in the early part of your life. None of it is wasted. Everything that came before is part of who you are today. It has taught you inadvertently and silently.

You are wise. You are seasoned. You are armed with enough wisdom to help you through anything life throws at you. This is what it means to be living *ahead of the curve.*

You are a wise woman now.

You can depend on it.

SELECTED BIBLIOGRAPHY

Babiak, Paul, Ph.D. & Robert D. Hare, Ph.D. *Snakes in Suits, When Psychopaths Go to Work.* New York: ReganBooks/ HarperCollins Publishers, Inc. 2006.

Blank, Joani. *Still Doing it. Women & Men over 60 Write About Their Sexuality.* San Francisco, CA: Down There Press. 2000.

Bortz, Walter M. II, M.D. *Dare To Be 100.* New York, NY: Fireside. 1996.

------. *We Live Too Short & Die Too Long, How to Achieve & Enjoy Your Natural 100-Year-Plus Life Span.* New York: Select Books, Inc. 2007.

Brody, Howard, M.D., Ph.D. *The Placebo Response.* New York, NY: Cliff Street Books. 2000.

Callan, Jamie Cat. *French Women Don't Sleep Alone.* New York, NY: Kensington Publishing Corp. 2009.

Carlson, Richard, Ph.D. *Shortcut Through Therapy, 10 Principles of Growth-Oriented, Contented Living.* New York: Plume/ Penguin Group. 1995.

Carrinton, Patricia, Ph.D. *Try It on Everything. Discover the Power of EFT.* Bethel, CT: Try It Productions. 2008.

Cialdini, Robert B., Ph.D. *The Psychology Influence of Persuasion.* New York, NY: William Morrow and Company, Inc. 1984.

Davidson, Sara. *Leap!: What Will We Do with the Rest of Our Lives?* New York: Random House Publishing Group. 2007.

Degette, Daina, Congresswoman. *Sex, Science & Stem Cells, Inside the Right Wing Assault on Reason.* Gilford, CT: The Lion Press. 2008.

Dyer, Dr. Wayne W. *The Power of Intention, Learning to Co-create Your World Your Way.* Carlsbad, CA: Hay House, Inc. 2004.

Ensler, Eve. *The Vagina Monologues.* New York: Villard Books/ Random House, Inc. 1998.

Ephron, Nora. *I Feel Bad About My Neck, and Other Thoughts on Being a Woman.* New York: Alfred A. Knoff. 2006.

Fishel, Deidre & Diana Holtzberg. *Still Doing It, The Intimate Lives of Women Over 60.* New York: Penguin Group. 2008.

Ford, Debbie. *Why Good People Do Bad Things, How to Stop Being Your Own Worst Enemy.* New York: HarperOne/HarperCollins Publisher. 2008.

Forleo, Marie. *Make Every Man Want You (or Make Yours Want You More).* New York: Present Perfect Press. 2005.

Friedan, Betty. *The Fountain of Age*. New York, NY: Simon & Schuster. 1993.

Friedman, Francine Pappadis. *MatchDotBomb. A Midlife Journey through Internet Dating*. Tuscon, AZ: Wheatmark. 2007.

Gaiwan, Shakti. *Creative Visualization*. San Rafael, CA: Bantam Books. 1978.

Gilbert, Elizabeth. *Eat, Pray, Love*. New York: Penguin Books. 2006.

Grabhorn, Lynn. *Excuse Me, Your Life is Waiting*. Charlottesville, VA: Hampton Roads Publishing Company, Inc. 2000.

Gray, John, Ph.D. *Mars & Venus on a Date*. New York: HarperCollins. 1997.

Hay, Louise L. *The Power is Within You*. Carson, CA: Hay House, Inc. 1991; *You Can Heal Your Life*. Carlsbad, CA: Hay House, Inc. 1987.

Hicks, Esther & Jerry Hicks. *The Law of Attraction, The Basics of the Teachings of Abraham*. United States: Hay House. 2008.

Humphry, Derek. *Final Exit*. Eugene, OR: The Hemlock Society. 1991.

Johnson, Spencer, M.D. *Who Moved My Cheese? An A-Mazing Way to Deal with Change in Your Work & in Your Life*. New York: G.P. Putnam's Sons. 1998.

Kerner, Ian, Ph.D. She Comes First, *The Thinking Man's Guide* to *Pleasuring a Woman*. New York: Regan Books/Harper-Collins Publishers, Inc. 2004.

Kingsolver, Barbara. *Animal, Vegetable, Miracle*. A Year of Food Life. New York: HarperCollins Publishers, Inc. 2007.

Klauser, Henriette Anne. *Write It Down, Make it Happen, Knowing What You Want–And Getting It!* New York: Touchstone/Simon & Schuster. 2000.

Klimo, Kate and Buffy Shutt. *Coming of Age... All Over Again*. New York: Spring Board Press/Hatchette Book Group USA. 2007.

Kliger, Leah, MHA, and Deborah Nedelman, Ph.D. *Still Sexy After All These Years? The 9 Unspoken Truths About Women's Desire Beyond 50*. New York: Perigee/The Penguin Group. 2006.

Krieger, Dolores, Ph.D., R.N. *Accepting Your Power to Heal. The Personal Practice of Therapeutic Touch*. Santa Fe, NM: Bear & Co. Publishing: 1993.

Linfield, Jordan L. and Joseph Krevisky. *Words of Love, Romantic Quotations from Plato to Madonna*. New York: Gramercy Books/Random House Value Publishing. 1997.

Lipton, Bruce H., Ph.D. *The Biology of Belief, Unleashing the Power of Consciousness, Matter & Miracles*. United States: Hay House, Inc. 2008.

Lusk, Julie T. *30 Scripts for Relaxation Imagery & Inner Healing*. Duluth, MN: Whole Person Associates. 1992

McTaggart, Lynne. *What Doctors Don't Tell You. The Truth*

About the Dangers of Modern Medicine. New York: Avon Books, Inc. 1998.

Millet, Catherine. *The Sexual Life of Catherine M.* New York: Grove Press Books. 2001.

Moran, Victoria. *Younger By the Day. 365 Ways to Rejuvinate Your Body & Revitalize Your Spirit.* New York: Harper Collins Publishers. 2004.

Moore, Myreah and Jodie Gould. *Date Like A Man. What Men Know About Dating & Are Afraid You'll Find Out.* New York: Quill/HarperCollins. 2000.

Myss, Caroline, Ph.D. *Why People Don't Heal And How They Can.* New York: Harmony Books. 1997.

Pert, Candace B. *The Molecules of Emotion: The Science Behind Mind-Body Medicine.* New York, NY: Touchstone. 1997.

Prochaska, James O., Ph.D., John C. Norcross, Ph.D., and Carlo C. DiClemente, Ph.D. *Changing For Good. A Revolutionary Six-Stage Program for Overcoming Bad Habits & Moving Your Life Positively Forward.* New York: HarperCollins. 1994.

Price, Joan. *Better Than I Ever Expected, Straight Talk About Sex After Sixty.* Emeryville, CA: Sea Press. 2006.

Propp, Karen and Jean Trounstine. *Why I'm Still Married.* New York, NY: Hudson Street Press. 2006.

Richardson, Cheryl. *Stand Up for Your Life.* New York: The Free Press. 2002.

Roach, Mary. *Bonk, The Curious Coupling of Science & Sex.* New York: W.W. Norton & Co. 2008.

Seligman, Martin E.P., Ph.D. *Authentic Happiness. Using the New Positive Psychology to Realize Your Potential for Lasting Fullfillment.* New York: Free Press/Simon & Schuster Inc. 2002.

Sheehy, Gail. *New Passages, Mapping Your Life Across Time.* New York: Ballantine Books/Random House Publishing Group. 1995.

St. James, Aleta. *Life Shift. Let Go & Live Your Dream.* New York: Fireside/Simon & Schulster. 2005.

Stoval, Jim. *The Ultimate Gift.* Colorado Springs, CO: David C. Cook. 2001.

Szereto, Mitzi. *The New Black Lace Book of Women's Sexual Fantasties.* London: Black Lace. 2008.

Tolle, Eckhart. *The Power of Now, A Guide to Spiritual Enlightenment.* Novato, CA: New World Library. 1999.

Trafford, Abigail. *My Time, Making the Most of the Bonus Decades AFTER FIFTY.* Cambrige, MA: Basic Books. 2004.

Trudeau, Kevin. *The Weight Loss Cure "They" Don't Want You to Know About.* Elk Grove Village, IL: Alliance Publishing Group. 2007.

Vitale, Joe. *The Attractor Factor.* Hoboken, NJ: John Wiley & Sons, Inc. 2008.

Whitworth, Laura, Karen Kimsey-House, Henry Kimsey-House, Phillip Sandahl. *Co-Active Coaching. New Skills for Coaching People Toward Success in Work & Life.* Mountain View, CA: Davies–Black Publishing/CPP. 2007.

LaVergne, TN USA
17 August 2009
155119LV00001B/3/P